PLOUGHSHA

Winter 1998–99 · Vol. 24, .

GUEST EDITOR
Thomas Lux

EDITOR
Don Lee

POETRY EDITOR
David Daniel

ASSISTANT EDITOR
Gregg Rosenblum

ASSOCIATE FICTION EDITOR
Maryanne O'Hara

ASSOCIATE POETRY EDITOR
Susan Conley

FOUNDING EDITOR
DeWitt Henry

FOUNDING PUBLISHER
Peter O'Malley

ADVISORY EDITORS

Russell Banks	DeWitt Henry	James Randall
Ann Beattie	Jane Hirshfield	Alberto Alvaro Ríos
Anne Bernays	Fanny Howe	Lloyd Schwartz
Frank Bidart	Marie Howe	Jane Shore
Robert Boswell	Justin Kaplan	Charles Simic
Rosellen Brown	Bill Knott	Gary Soto
James Carroll	Yusef Komunyakaa	Maura Stanton
Madeline DeFrees	Maxine Kumin	Gerald Stern
Rita Dove	Philip Levine	Mark Strand
Andre Dubus	Thomas Lux	Christopher Tilghman
Stuart Dybek	Gail Mazur	Richard Tillinghast
Carolyn Forché	James Alan McPherson	Chase Twichell
Richard Ford	Leonard Michaels	Fred Viebahn
George Garrett	Sue Miller	Ellen Bryant Voigt
Lorrie Goldensohn	Lorrie Moore	Dan Wakefield
Mary Gordon	Jay Neugeboren	Derek Walcott
David Gullette	Howard Norman	James Welch
Marilyn Hacker	Tim O'Brien	Alan Williamson
Donald Hall	Joyce Peseroff	Tobias Wolff
Paul Hannigan	Jayne Anne Phillips	Al Young
Stratis Haviaras	Robert Pinsky	

PLOUGHSHARES, a journal of new writing, is guest-edited serially by prominent writers who explore different and personal visions, aesthetics, and literary circles. PLOUGHSHARES is published in April, August, and December at Emerson College, 100 Beacon Street, Boston, MA 02116-1596. Telephone: (617) 824-8753. Web address: www.emerson.edu/ploughshares.

EDITORIAL ASSISTANTS: Kris Fikkan, Eson Kim, Michelle Campo, and Jean Hopkinson. STAFF ASSISTANT: Tom Herd.

POETRY READERS: Brian Scales, Jennifer Thurber, Tom Laughlin, Jessica Purdy, Michael J. Carter, Renee Rooks, Charlotte Pence, R. J. Lavallee, and Paul Berg.

FICTION READERS: Scott Clavenna, Monique Hamzé, Karen Wise, Emily Doherty, Leah Stewart, Tammy Zambo, Mary Jeanne Deery, Jeffrey Freiert, Jessica Olin, Michael Rainho, Gregg Rosenblum, Darla Bruno, Laurel Santini, Billie Lydia Porter, and Elizabeth Pease.

SUBSCRIPTIONS (ISSN 0048-4474): $21 for one year (3 issues), $40 for two years (6 issues); $24 a year for institutions. Add $5 a year for international.

UPCOMING: Spring 1999, a poetry and fiction issue edited by Mark Doty, will appear in April 1999. Fall 1999, a fiction issue edited by Charles Baxter, will appear in August 1999.

SUBMISSIONS: Reading period is from August 1 to March 31 (postmark dates). Please see page 238 for detailed submission policies.

Back-issue, classroom-adoption, and bulk orders may be placed directly through PLOUGHSHARES. Authorization to photocopy journal pieces may be granted by contacting PLOUGHSHARES for permission and paying a fee of 25¢ per page, per copy. Microfilms of back issues may be obtained from University Microfilms. PLOUGHSHARES is also available as CD-ROM and full-text products from EBSCO, H.W. Wilson, Information Access, and UMI. Indexed in M.L.A. Bibliography, American Humanities Index, Index of American Periodical Verse, Book Review Index. Self-index through Volume 6 available from the publisher; annual supplements appear in the fourth number of each subsequent volume. The views and opinions expressed in this journal are solely those of the authors. All rights for individual works revert to the authors upon publication.

PLOUGHSHARES receives support from the Lannan Foundation, the National Endowment for the Arts, and the Massachusetts Cultural Council.

Retail distribution by Bernhard DeBoer (Nutley, NJ), Ingram Periodicals (La Vergne, TN), and Koen Book Distributors (Moorestown, NJ).

Printed in the U.S.A. on recycled paper by Edwards Brothers.

© 1998 by Emerson College

CONTENTS

Winter 1998–99

Cover painting by Mathew R. Weaver
Acrylic on paper, 22″ x 30″, 1996

Ploughshares
Patrons

This nonprofit publication would not be possible without the
support of our readers and the generosity of the following
individuals and organizations. An additional list of donor
acknowledgements may be found on page 243.

COUNCIL
Denise and Mel Cohen
Eugenia Gladstone Vogel
Marillyn Zacharis

PATRONS
Anonymous
Jacqueline Liebergott
Estate of Charles T. Robb
Turow Foundation

FRIENDS
Johanna Cinader
In Memory of Larry Levis

ORGANIZATIONS
Emerson College
Lannan Foundation
Massachusetts Cultural Council
National Endowment for the Arts

COUNCIL: $3,000 for two lifetime subscriptions,
acknowledgement in the journal for three years,
and votes on the Cohen and Zacharis Awards.
PATRON: $1,000 for a lifetime subscription and
acknowledgement in the journal for two years.
FRIEND: $500 for a lifetime subscription and
acknowledgement in the journal for one year.
All donations are tax-deductible.
Please make your check payable to
Ploughshares, Emerson College,
100 Beacon St., Boston, MA 02116.

THOMAS LUX

Introduction

In a brief introduction to the last issue of *Ploughshares* I guest-edited (Spring 1985, Vol. 11, No. 1), I noted that nearly twelve years had passed since the first issue I edited (Summer 1973, Vol. 1, No. 4) and that I'd be happy to do it again in another dozen years or so. Blink: a dozen years or so.

Even though this isn't a "discovery" issue, you will find, among several well-known poets and fiction writers, many newer or younger writers, some appearing for the first time in a national magazine. I solicited poems and stories and an interview from writers whose work I know and like, but much more came in over the transom. This was one of the real pleasures in editing this issue. May the reader's pleasure be half as great as mine.

If I'm lucky enough to reach the average age men die (about seventy-five) in our culture and maintain my current pace (and providing *Ploughshares* management *asks* me again), I should be able to do this two more times, say around 2010 and 2022. I do not advise holding your breath. I do hope, however, that some of these poems and stories, or the essay or interview, take your breath away.

CHRIS ADRIAN

The Sum of Our Parts

B eatrice needed a new liver. Her old one had succumbed to damage suffered in a fall one month earlier from the top of a seven-story parking garage. She lay in a coma while the hospital prepared for her imminent transplant, but she was not asleep. That part of her which was not her broken body stood by her bed in the surgical intensive care unit and watched as a nurse leaned over to draw her blood.

Beatrice's unusual condition gave her access to aspects of people which usually are utterly private. So she knew that the nurse, whose name was Judy, was thinking of her husband. It was eleven-thirty p.m., just about his bedtime, and Judy imagined him settling down to sleep. He would take off his shirt and his pants and fold the sheet down neatly so it covered him to just past his hips. He would turn on his side and put a hand under his cheek. Judy missed acutely the space between his shoulder blades, into which she was accustomed to settling her face as she waited for sleep to come.

Distracted, she missed the vein, and cursed softly when she noticed that no blood came into the tube. Beatrice's body lay unprotesting as Judy shifted the needle beneath her skin, questing after the already sorely-abused vein. Beatrice did not feel it when Judy found the vein and the borrowed blood (in the first hours of her stay Beatrice had received a complete transfusion) slipped quietly into a red-topped tube. When that one was full Judy proceeded to fill a gray-topped tube, a lavender-topped tube, and finally a tube with a rubber stopper the color of freshly-laid robin's eggs.

Judy straightened up and stared at her patient as her hands went automatically about the business of attaching red-numbered labels to the tubes. Beatrice was a medium-sized woman with rich curly red hair but otherwise unremarkable features. Beneath obscuring tubes and wires, her skin was pale and slightly greenish, and under her spare hospital nightie her once generous form was getting bony. In the same way, her hair was not so lovely as it had been on her admission, when it was bright and coppery. Now it was duller, though still pretty, and at the roots it had darkened to a muddy, bloody color. As she wrapped the tubes in a laboratory requisition form and tucked the little package into a plastic bag, Judy resolved to come back and give Beatrice's hair a full one hundred strokes of brushing. This seemed to Beatrice, who no longer cared about her hair, a waste of time.

The blood neatly and safely organized, and all her sharps-waste disposed of, Judy turned on her heel and walked out of the semi-private recess that Beatrice occupied in the first bay of the SICU. Judy walked down the bay, nodding at the nurses and doctors whose eyes she caught. Beatrice followed her out. She was nodding at people, too. No one saw her.

Judy walked up to the front desk, where a perpetually idle nursing assistant named Frank was flipping through an old issue of *Reader's Digest* and looking bored.

"Here you go," she said, pushing the blood at him. "Take this up to the lab and tell them it's extra-stat."

"Sure thing," he said, closing his magazine. He took the blood from her and felt a familiar wave of dislike pass over him. Mouse-face, he thought to himself. Others in the SICU agreed with him that Judy had mousy features: a small, forward-sloping face beset with a long, thin nose; prominent, well-cared-for front teeth. Whenever Judy was in a mood and taking it out on the other nursing staff, he would whisper to one of his friends, "Perhaps the rodent would like a piece of cheese." He had not gone so far as to leave a piece of cheddar in her locker, but he planned to do that one day.

The thought of her expression as she beheld the cheese sitting on top of her street shoes, and the thought that followed that one, of her bending down with alacrity and nibbling it up, amused him greatly. He laughed out loud on his way out of the bay, even as another nurse hurried up to him with a full gallon jug of urine to carry up to the lab. Beatrice, who did not find any of the mouse business amusing, and did not particularly care for Frank, followed him out of the SICU, walking just a few steps behind him and watching as he swung the jug of urine back and forth and hummed to himself.

Walking down the wide hospital hallway, Frank looked out the enormous windows on his right. Outside it was snowing, but he could just barely see that. What the windows showed him was mainly his own reflection. Looking at himself, he regretted not wearing a shirt beneath his scrubs, because he thought the cut of his sleeves made his arms look thin and weak.

He took the elevator labeled EE up to the sixth floor, not noticing that Beatrice had stepped in behind him. On the sixth floor he walked straight out of the elevator and down a hall that looked over a balcony into an atrium whose main feature was a shiny black grand piano. The atrium extended in a shaft up through every floor of the hospital. Sometimes people came in and played something cheery on the piano, but never during his shift. Beatrice had heard them during the day. Her favorite was a little Mennonite girl who sat primly under her paper hat and played hymns. Turning right, away from the hallway, Frank and Beatrice entered the demesne of the pathology department.

Frank was always surprised by how nice it smelled there, not at all like a hospital, or even like a lab. There were no foul odors like what proceeded from people with failed kidneys, nor any sharp chemical smells to make your nose itch. Rather, the lab smelled like the perfume of the beautiful women who worked there. To Beatrice it smelled sweet also, mostly because there were people there whom she counted as friends, though none of them had ever met her. The lab was one of her favorite places to spend time.

Frank had a passing interest in one of Beatrice's friends, a blue-eyed hematology technologist with poor dental hygiene but very handsome hips. His name was Denis. He wasn't there when Frank dropped off the blood and urine. Two women and one man were intent on their computer screens, typing in various patient information, ordering tests, and entering results. They did not notice Frank in the window.

"Stat!" Frank shouted, and had a feeling like a smile in his belly when they all jumped. Beatrice wanted to smack him.

"Thank you," said the man, a funny-looking, taciturn fellow with enormous ears. "You can leave it there."

"It's super-stat," said Frank, setting the urine in the window.

"All right," said the man.

"We need you to get right on it. This lady's getting her transplant started in the morning."

"Right," said one of the women, who was thin with long straight hair. Frank envied her her eyes, which were green and gold. She rolled her chair over to the window and snatched the blood from his hand.

"Thank you," she said, setting the tubes next to her computer terminal but doing nothing with them. Her name was Bonnie. She made a show of being focused on her screen, waiting for Frank to go away. Go away, she thought, exerting the full force of her will upon the odious nursing assistant. Beatrice tried to help her out and wished fervently that Frank would return to his hell of shrewish nurses.

"He's gone," said the man with the ears. His name was Luke.

"I can't stand the way that guy looks at me," said Bonnie, adroitly unwrapping the blood, unfolding the requisition, and entering the requested tests into the computer.

"Like a snake," said Olivia, the other woman.

"Damn!" said Bonnie. She'd noticed that the urine had no name on it. She stuck her head out the window and called down the hall, "Hey, urine boy!" If Frank heard, he made no response.

"What's wrong?" asked Luke.

"They didn't label the urine. What a pain in my ass."

"I'll call them," he said.

"Thanks," Bonnie said. She watched Luke as he got up and walked over to the phone, wondering why he always cut his hair so short instead of leaving it long to cover his silly ears. They really are very large, she thought, and wondered if that signified anything, in terms of personality. Men with large hands were said to possess large penises, red-haired people were said to be volatile, but she had never heard anything special said about people with large ears, except maybe that they heard a little better than most folks. Someone might have told her that, maybe her grandmother or her sixth-grade science teacher. To Beatrice, Luke's ears indicated oafishness, because her big-eared father had been a great oaf. But regardless of the ears, Beatrice found herself partial to Luke.

Luke hung up the phone and said, "They're sending it up." Behind him self-adhesive labels were printing out for Beatrice's specimens. Bonnie looked him up and down again, and thought about how she might have found him attractive in some other lifetime, one with different standards of beauty. For what seemed to her the hundredth time she imagined him shirtless and was disappointed. She got up from her chair and handed the specimens to Olivia. "Would you label these, please?" she asked.

"Sure," she said. "Hey, it's the jumping lady!"

"Is it?" said Bonnie. "I didn't notice."

"I wonder how she's doing," said Luke.

"Not too well," said Bonnie, "if she needs a new liver."

"But as well as can be expected," said Olivia. "I mean, considering." She was labeling intently.

"You really should wear gloves when you do that," said Luke.

"I know," said Olivia.

"One of the tubes might break in your hand. Then where would you be?"

"All bloody," said Bonnie. "I know. It happened to me once. Lucky I had gloves on."

"Would you like me to put on some gloves?" Olivia asked Luke.

"I don't care," he said. "It was just a suggestion."

"Jesus," said Olivia. Beatrice came through the window and stood next to her. You have nothing to fear from my blood, she said, but Olivia did not hear her.

Olivia was, in fact, wishing she had put on a pair of gloves. She smoothed a label onto the round edges of a lavender-topped tube and suffered from the perversity of her imagination. She imagined the tube breaking in half as she held it, the jagged glass edge piercing her thumb to the bone, inoculating her with the jumping lady's blood and whatever diseases it carried. In the same way she sometimes imagined being a bystander in a bank robbery, standing behind a security guard when he got shot with such force that the bullet passed right through him and into her. Who could tell what she might get? Who could speculate on the habits of that security guard, and whether or not they spelled death for her?

Olivia shook her head and walked the blood through the lab, back into the chemistry section, where Otto, the great big chemistry technologist, sat with his feet up on the Hitachi 747, a very accomplished machine that was capable of all sorts of magnificently complex chemical analyses of serum and plasma, as well as urine and cerebrospinal fluid, and even stool, provided it was of a sufficiently liquid consistency. Beatrice had followed right behind her, and now she watched as Olivia watched the sleeping Otto, admiring his strong jaw. Olivia was committed to a girl she'd met in her organic chemistry class, but she felt no guilt admiring Otto's jaw, or any other portion of his vast anatomy.

"Wake up," she said, putting the red- and the gray-topped tubes in a rack by Otto's foot. She wiggled the tip of his shoe with her hand.

"I'm not sleeping," he said. "Just resting my eyes."

"Sure," she said. "You're not allowed to be tired yet. We've got seven more hours."

Otto sat up, picked up the tubes, and began to transfer them to his centrifuge. "Oh," he said. "It's the jumping lady."

"Yup." Olivia walked off towards the hematology section of the lab, then turned back. "I guess you can take some of this for the ammonia level," she said, offering him the lavender-topped tube. "But give it to Denis as soon as you're done."

"Sure," he said. "Thanks." The thought of having an excuse to go in search of Denis appealed to him. He felt the same way about Denis that Frank and Bonnie did.

As quickly as he could, he pulled off a small aliquot of Beatrice's blood and put it into a small plastic test tube. He was careless in his haste; a single gorgeous drop fell and landed on his ungloved index finger. Panic flared in him because he thought for a moment that he had a raw hangnail on that finger, but it was actually on the index finger of the other hand. Nevertheless he hurried to the sink and sprayed bleach from a squeeze bottle onto his finger. The smell reminded him of the bathroom he grew up with, which his mother had religiously disinfected, practically after every use. Beatrice stood next to him and said, You have nothing to fear from my blood.

When he was all cleaned up, Otto got the ammonia level and other analyses running in the 747 and hurried down to hematology. He found Denis hunched over a magazine full of details about the lives of musicians. Denis looked up when Otto rounded the −70° freezer.

"Hi," he said. Beatrice came in, sat on the freezer, and began to drum her legs silently against its side.

"Hi, there," said Otto, gazing not at Denis's hips but at the upper portion of his biceps. Those muscles appealed to him not because they were particularly large (they were only about a third the size of his own) but because they were very shapely, and because he could very well imagine himself drifting off to sleep with his cheek resting against them.

"What's up?" Denis asked.

"Got some blood for you. They want a CBC and a diff and a sed rate."

"No problem." Denis held his hand out for the tube. Otto placed it in his palm, taking care despite himself not to let any part of his hand touch Denis, but his pinkie scraped Denis's wrist as he drew his hand away.

"It's the jumping lady," said Otto.

"Oh," said Denis. His placid expression belied his true reaction. He thought he could feel his heart rising in his chest, and he wanted to bring the blood to his forehead and hold it there, but of course he didn't. Otto was standing in front of him, looking down and smiling awkwardly.

"Looks like she's getting a transplant," he said.

"Another one?"

"Liver this time." The previous one had been a kidney.

"Where do they get all these organs?"

Otto shrugged. "Got to get to work," he said, walking away. The phone rang. Denis picked it up and listened for a few moments, then hung up and walked out into the hall. He could see Otto down past the other end, bending over his machine. "Hey, Otto!" he said. "The liver's on its way! They're sending up some donor blood for serology!"

"Okay!" Otto shouted back. Denis walked back to his lab, sat down, and began to work. He felt very strongly about the jumping lady. It was his conviction that he was in love with her, and had been ever since she had first arrived, ever since he had heard her story and handled her blood for the first time. He closed his magazine and sighed. He leaned his head against the machine that was busy counting and sorting her blood cells by type, waiting for the information, which was precious to him because it concerned her.

Beatrice sat and watched him, feeling sad because if she was in love with anyone in the lab, it was not Denis, and was probably nobody, but just might be Luke of the enormous ears. She could not bear to watch Denis mooning over her, so she left his lab through an open back door and headed up to the roof, where she waited in the blowing snow for the arrival of her new liver.

She looked out on the city from a familiar height. The hospital, like the parking garage, was seven stories tall. She could see the university campus spread out before her, neatly bisected by the river. When she tried to leave, she got only as far as that river. Some force held her bound to the hospital. She supposed it was her living body, and wished it would die. It was not for no reason at all that she threw herself off the garage. Not that she could recall the reason, in her present state. She only knew that she did not wish to go back, and that it all had to do with a crushing sadness that under which she had labored for most of her life, and which she had never blamed on anybody.

She heard the helicopter before she saw it. It was incredibly loud. Covering her ears with her hands, she watched as it came out of the snowstorm and settled onto the helipad. She watched the flight nurses scramble out, one of them with a Styrofoam cooler held between his hands. Just as they had with the kidney, they would take it downstairs, where doctors would examine it and make it ready for her. After the nurses had disappeared inside the hospital, Beatrice turned and stepped off the roof.

It was never like the fall that had brought her here. It was slower, for one thing, and it did her no harm whatsoever. In fact, she fell so slowly that she had time for reflection on various subjects, and this time as she floated down, she watched the snowflakes passing her and thought about her very first boyfriend. His name was Boukman. They had been eight years old together. Her parents had disapproved of him because he was black. They would not let him swim in their pool. This was in Miami, where in the summer it was practically a medical necessity to swim every day.

So she swam in his family's pool, and exulted in his strangeness. Boukman claimed to have been born of a dog, and that he could fly. These were not his parents who applauded when he and she did synchronized back dives into the pool. His real mother's name was Queenie, and she was a Great Dane just like Scooby Doo. He was from Haiti. He said such things were common there. She believed him all through the summer, and looked forward to the flying lessons he promised her.

On the day of the first lesson, she gave him a lingering kiss on the mouth, and then they ran hand in hand along his flat roof.

She balked at the edge and watched him go flying out alone. He went out and straight down to fall directly on his well-formed, closely shaven head. She looked down at the gruesome angle of his neck. Because she was a child, she did not realize right away that he was dead.

In later years she wondered if it had been her doubt which cost him his life. If she had jumped with him, would they have flown over all the low houses of their respectable neighborhood, and scraped their toes against the tops of the highest royal palms? It seemed unlikely.

As she approached the ground, Beatrice realized that Boukman was not the great sadness of her life. It was not for him that she had made her leap, though she would always think of him as the beginning of a long arc of sadness, as the person who taught her that there's no such thing as a boy who can fly, and that nothing is born of a dog but puppies and blood.

Beatrice walked into the ER, following behind a pair of EMTs who were wheeling in a motorcycle accident victim. The few people in the waiting room looked up as the man was pushed past them. He was crying out, "Louise! Louise!" at the top of his lungs. Beatrice watched as they rushed him down the hall to the trauma center. Snow swirled in around her before the doors closed again, and the waiting people went back to staring absently at their entertainment magazines or the television. Walking unseen through the restricted area, Beatrice could hear people having their various emergencies behind the curtains that separated the exam beds. She did not pause to look at the shattered kneecaps or the scalp wounds, or the blue and gray asthmatics wheezing desperately. She walked as quickly as she could, trying to catch up with the flight nurses who were carrying her liver up to surgery.

She didn't catch them. Her fall had given them a long start on her. But somewhere near the cardiovascular intensive care unit she happened upon Olivia, who was striding confidently down the hall carrying a phlebotomy basket and singing "Maria." Beatrice followed her clear across the hospital to the nurseries, where Olivia had been called to perform a blood draw on a brand-new baby. Olivia did not mind being called to do phlebotomy. In fact, she liked very much to escape the confines of the lab, but sometimes it disturbed her to have to cause an infant pain, even if it was for its own good. They entered the nursery and saw a large nurse rocking and feeding a baby. The flesh of the nurse's thighs spilled out from under the armrests of her rocking chair. "There she is," she said, pointing to a warming bed in a far corner of the room. Beatrice took a moment to admire the cheery decorations: rabbits and ponies and kittens, and a fine triptych of three dogs under a candy bush. The first dog's eyes were big as saucers, the second's as big as dessert plates, and the third's as big as dinner plates. This last picture made Beatrice feel sad.

Next to the warming bed, Olivia was preparing the baby for her blood draw.

"Hello, darling," she said. "You're so beautiful!" She scrubbed vigorously at the baby's foot with an alcohol-soaked cotton ball. The baby found this a not-unpleasant sensation. Olivia, full of regret, unwrapped a lancet from its sterile foil package and drove it mercilessly into the fleshiest part of the baby's heel.

"Sorry, darling," said Olivia. The baby, who did not yet have a name but would one day be called Sylvia, did not immediately begin to scream. First a look of perfect incredulity passed over her small face. Only when that had been replaced with an expression of righteous outrage did she begin to scream with such force and volume that Beatrice thought it would blow Olivia's hair back like a hot wind.

"Yes, yes," said Olivia. "Life is hard. Don't I know it?" This is only the beginning, Beatrice whispered behind her.

Olivia had caught the heel in the well between her thumb and forefinger, and now she began to squeeze with the full force of her hand. Sometimes Olivia thought she heard the heel bone making crunching noises under the pressure, but Bonnie had assured her that it was all in her head, and that it was quite impossible to crush a baby's heel because the bones were so fresh and green.

A dark red pearl of blood had formed from out of the wound, but Olivia wiped this away with a piece of gauze because it was too full of clotting factors to be useful for analysis. She continued squeezing, and caught the next drop in a tiny plastic tube, and the next drop, and then the next. She counted twenty-five of them before she had collected the requisite two hundred and fifty microliters.

It took a very long time. The blood was slow to come. Olivia began to experience misery because of the heat lamps that kept the chilly babies warm like so many hamburgers. There was a lamp in the roof of the warming bed, directly above Olivia's neck where she bent over the baby. She wished for an assistant to wipe away the sweat from her brow before it dripped down onto the baby. Beatrice would have been happy to help her, if she could have.

"Like the Sahara under there, isn't it?" said the fat nurse, who was watching Olivia sweat.

"I think I'm getting dehydrated," said Olivia, squeezing out the final drop. She capped her tube and put a festive adhesive bandage across the heel. The baby continued to scream, even though both Olivia and Beatrice stroked her arms and belly to try and calm her. Even after they were gone out the door she screamed. Beatrice lingered at the observation window and watched the beet-red baby writhe and scream while the cooing blob of a nurse burped her nursery mate. Beatrice put à hand on the window and said, It only gets worse and worse and worse.

When they got back to the lab, Beatrice and Olivia found the others clustered around a table, getting ready to draw each other's blood. Bonnie looked up at Olivia from where she sat with her bare arm spread out before her.

"How'd it go?" she asked.

"Tough. That baby had blood like glue, but I got it."

"Congratulations. Have you seen a blue-top floating around? Denis says he's missing one. He's all upset."

"I thought we got one on the jumping lady. I know I labeled one."

"Well, he didn't get it. I guess it's with Jesus now."

"Want to get drawn?" asked Otto.

"Sure," said Olivia. "Just let me get this back to Denis."

"Bring him back with you!" Bonnie called out after her. Beatrice stayed behind and watched as Luke stroked the crook of Bonnie's arm with his gloved hand, trying to get the vein to rise.

"Hurry up," Bonnie said. "This tourniquet is killing me."

"Sorry," he said. "I think I have it now." Beatrice stood next to him and observed closely as he slipped the needle into Bonnie's vein. His motion was certain and swift. Bonnie, looking away like she always did when she got her blood drawn, did not even notice the entry.

"We haven't got all night, you know," she said.

"Yeah," said Luke, biting his lip as he pushed a vacuum-filled test tube up into the plastic sheath that covered the bottom of the needle. Inside the sheath was the sharpened back end of the needle, and they could all hear a dull popping sound as it broke the vacuum in the tube. Beatrice watched, fascinated, as Bonnie's living blood beat into the tube. She imagined herself in Bonnie's place, imagined Luke's sure fingers caressing the crook of her arm. She stood closer to him and pretended that the growing erection that shamed and disturbed him was inspired by her. He pulled out the needle and pressed a pad of gauze against the wound.

"You big smoothie," said Bonnie. "I didn't even notice."

"That's the idea," said Luke. "Who wants to draw me?" He hoped it would be Bonnie, but she was absorbed by her own blood, holding the tube up to the fluorescent light from the ceiling and swirling the contents.

"I can never believe how red it is," she said.

"Sit down, Luke," said Otto. "I'll take care of you."

Otto put on a pair of extra-large gloves and proceeded to draw Luke's blood. He used a new needle, but Luke almost wished Otto would use the same one he had used on Bonnie. That would be a certain type of closeness, he thought.

Olivia came up behind them with Denis just in time to observe the penetration. As she watched Otto execute a flawless phlebotomy procedure, she imagined him, with his swollen muscles and great strength, driving the needle straight through Luke's arm and out the other side.

"You're getting good at this, Otto," she said, patting him on the back. She left her arm resting on the back of his shoulder and felt the subtle workings in the great muscle as he switched tubes, then finished the draw.

"Thanks," he said. He drew her next, then Denis. It was something of a thrill to watch Denis roll up his sleeve and expose the vein that stood out in bold relief all the way down his arm. As he felt the vein under his thumb, he imagined his own heart beating in exact time with Denis's, then had a vision of their two bodies, especially the chests, pressed up against each other, and both of them marveling at the synchronicity of their hearts as they held each other.

When he was finished, Otto sat down and tried to roll up his sleeve, but he could only get it as far as his upper forearm. Beyond that, his arm was too thick for the cuff, so he was forced to remove his shirt. Beatrice stood by Denis as he performed the draw, and admired the pattern of black hair that spread from Otto's belly up his abdomen, over his chest, and under his arms. It looked soft and well cared for, as if he used expensive shampoo on it instead of soap. She wanted to touch it, so she did.

Olivia admired it, too, fiercely, and pictured her face against it, and even went so far as to position herself next to Otto to see if she could catch a scent from under his elevated arm. Bonnie found herself appreciative of the flat lines of Otto's stomach, and the wide stretch of his chest, and especially the thick, wing-like extension of the muscles along his sides. Luke watched Bonnie watching Otto, and envied him. Denis thought solely of his jumping lady.

He thought of her lying in the OR, perhaps already opened up, and prayed silently that her operation would come off without any complications. Beatrice muttered a prayer of her own to thwart Denis's: she prayed for a power outage or an incompetent anesthetist or that someone would drop the liver.

She waited a little longer in the lab, while Denis and Otto performed the analyses on all the blood, because she wanted to make sure her friends were healthy. It turned out that Luke's iron level could have been higher and that Bonnie's glucose was dreadfully low.

"Time for lunch!" Bonnie said when she learned this, and went to go find Denis to convince him to help her hunt down the traveling food cart. Luke watched her go, then picked up the phone because it was ringing. He listened with a grave expression, and said, "All right," then hung up. He folded his arms across his chest and said to Olivia, who was busy entering results into the computer, "Transplant's canceled. The jumping lady is dead."

Beatrice, upon hearing this, did not stay to see Olivia's reaction, but made directly for the river.

She was severely disappointed when she realized that she still could not pass over the bridge. She puzzled over this the whole way back to the hospital. She wondered, Will I be stuck here forever? She went looking for her body.

When she found it her questions were answered. It was still in the SICU, though now in a different room. Outside she saw a team of doctors arguing with each other. "What am I supposed to do with this liver?" one of them wanted to know.

Another doctor was interrogating Judy, who felt close to weeping with frustration. She repeated her story, that Beatrice had coded while she was brushing her hair.

"And who told you to go around brushing people on their hair?" a doctor asked her. He was from Iran. Judy had never liked him.

"For God's sake, I was trying to be nice!" said Judy. "And if you don't like that you can just fuck yourself right out of the profession!" She turned and stormed away, damning the consequences of her outburst. As she ran out of the bay, Frank turned to a fellow nursing assistant and said, "The mouse roars." Beatrice went and looked at her body.

This was not the first time that her body had experienced a spontaneous and universal shutdown of organ systems, but every other time somebody had revived it. Her body looked the same to Beatrice as it ever did, but she knew from the conversation around her that she was certifiably brain dead. Now machines gave her a semblance of life, keeping her unruined organs alive for transplant to someone else.

Beatrice turned away from her body and wandered out of the bay. It would be a while before they took her off the machine and began to remove her organs. There were blood tests to run, and the organ harvesting team would need to be roused from their beds. She went and found her liver, still waiting for her in the OR. It was the sole occupant of the room. She went and looked at it where it lay in a volume of pale pink fluid that was not blood. But the whole thing reeked so strongly of blood that she thought she might faint.

"Be happy, liver," she said to it, and went back up to the pathology lab because she wanted to spend her last hours at the hospital among friends.

Halfway back to the lab she heard music and followed it. It took her downstairs, through many different hallways, always sounding very close because the acoustics in this part of the hospital were strange. It was not unusual for a stray groan to come floating down the hall to disturb a candystriper on some innocuous mission.

The music led her to the third-floor balcony over the atrium, where she looked down and saw Bonnie playing on the big piano while Denis sat glumly beside her. Bonnie played sprightly in a high octave and sang:

> *Fingers are fun,*
> *Toes are nice,*
> *Brains are soft*
> *And gray like mice*
> *But blood is best.*
>
> *Yes blood is the best,*
> *Oh blood is the best,*
> *Even your mama will tell you*
> *That blood is the best because*
> *Blood is the sum of our parts.*

She stopped singing but continued to play softly. "My mother the nurse taught me that song. A crazy lady in housekeeping taught it to her. She—the housekeeper, not my mother—got fired for sipping clotted blood out of used specimen tubes. Said it tasted like oysters." Bonnie was trying to amuse Denis because he was so sad. When she went back to ask him to lunch, he was just putting down his phone. He stood frozen over his machines for a moment, then burst violently into tears. For a moment Bonnie was uncertain what to do, but then she ran to him and threw her arms around him, saying, "It's okay, Denis," which was the first thing she could think of.

Denis didn't particularly want to be held. He hated Bonnie briefly, because she was alive and the jumping lady was dead, and if in that moment he could have traded one life for the other, he certainly would have. Bonnie held him, and he cried into her lab-coated shoulder for a few minutes, then stood back from her. "I don't know what's wrong with me," he said.

"It's been a long night," she said, though it hadn't, really. It had been almost relaxing, so far, because it was so slow. I'm holding him! she thought. What else matters?

"It's the jumping lady," he said. "She's dead. It's sad."

"I didn't know!" Bonnie exclaimed. "I didn't know you knew her!"

"I didn't," he said. "It's just sad, is all." A fresh sob rose up from his belly and burst out of his mouth.

Bonnie looked over Denis's shoulder and saw Luke staring at them from the hall. He turned and walked away. "Let's get out of here for a minute," she said, taking him by the hand and leading him out the back door. He did not protest, even as she led all the way to the piano, sat him down there, and began to play.

Above them, while Bonnie moved her fingers over the lowest section of the keyboard and started a new song, Beatrice stepped off the balcony and began to float down. She managed a perfect landing on the piano, and sat down cross-legged on it, staring intently into the faces of Bonnie and Denis, who were not looking at each other. Bonnie stopped playing.

"Are you feeling better?"

"Sure," said Denis. "Thanks. It's weird how it got to me like that." He did not plan ever to tell anyone that he had been in love with the jumping lady.

"I think it's a good thing," she said. "You'd make a good doctor."

"No thanks." A nearby elevator opened its doors, and a security guard emerged from it. He approached them warily.

"You're not allowed to be playing that piano," he said.

"Yeah, right," said Bonnie. "Whatever." She launched into "Chopsticks."

"I'm going to have to ask you to stop that."

"If you want me to stop, you're going to have to shoot me," said Bonnie.

"Maybe we should be going," said Denis.

"I'm enjoying myself," said Bonnie. "Is it a crime to enjoy yourself in a hospital? Are people allowed only to suffer and die here?" She began to play "Für Elise." The guard peered at their nametags and made notes in a small black book.

"We're on our way," said Denis, pulling at Bonnie's arm.

"I'll have to file an incident report," the guard said.

"File away!" said Bonnie. She felt giddy. Perhaps it was the after-effect of having Denis in her arms, or of being next to him.

"I'll see you up in the lab," said Denis. He got up and walked away. She stopped playing and walked after him.

"Wait!" she said. "Let's go find the food cart." The guard walked away, thinking of all the patients wanting their sleep. Beatrice remained on top of the piano. She lay on her back and looked up all the way to the top of the atrium, seven stories up. She saw people walking by occasionally, along the balconies, carrying blood to the lab or moving a patient. She saw the beautiful Filipino woman who worked in the dietary department wheeling the third-shift food cart along the balcony and eating a candy bar.

She closed her eyes and imagined all her friends from the lab standing spread out on all the different levels and balconies while she herself floated above the piano. She imagined them calling out to each other: Olivia to Otto, Otto to Denis, Denis to her, she to Luke, Luke to Bonnie, and Bonnie to Denis. They were all shouting, "Please love me."

When she returned to the lab, Beatrice found it in chaos. The respite they'd been enjoying was over, and things were very busy again. She sat in the window and watched Luke as he rushed around, looking hapless.

He felt lost in a rush of fluid. They were getting tests now not just for blood but for urine, and CSF, and all manner of effusions. Nursing assistants came and dumped specimens in great quantities at the window. There were even small pieces of people coming up now, discreet bits of organ or tumor to be processed and frozen for a pathologist to look at in the morning. Someone dropped off a whole human brain in a Tupperware container full of formaldehyde.

And there was much stool, most of it quite runny, packaged in blue plastic containers that looked to Luke much like the containers in which delis packaged their potato salad. In the hurry to get things done, he dropped one. He was acutely grateful that it didn't break open on the floor. Instead it bounced and rolled, coming to rest nestled against Olivia's shoe.

"Sorry," he said.

"That's okay." Olivia suffered another moment of perversity in which she imagined picking up the container and throwing its soupy contents all over Luke, and all over the walls and windows of the lab, all the while shouting, "Shit! Shit! Shit!"

"I'm getting very tired," she said.

"Tell me about it," he said. Much time had passed, though Luke barely noticed. It was almost five. He could go home at six. They all could, but he wasn't looking particularly forward to it. He wondered if one day he and Bonnie might leave together and go to his apartment. Otto wandered up from the chemistry lab.

"Make it stop," he said. "I don't want to work anymore."

"I think it's slowing down," said Luke.

"Where's Bonnie?" Otto asked, sitting down at one of the empty terminals.

"In the back," said Olivia. "With Denis." It was a quality of her perpetually sweaty palms that they made a sucking sound when ground together and rapidly pulled apart. She made those sounds now, and winked. In fact Bonnie was only helping Denis do differential cell counts. He had forgiven her for causing a scene, and she had been so bold as to make plans with him for later in the day.

"I'll be right back," said Luke. He walked out of the lab, down the hall, and into the men's bathroom. Beatrice followed right behind. She watched him at the urinal, craning her head around his side to get a glimpse of his penis. It was not very exciting, and she realized with a very mild sort of sadness that she did not really desire him physically. Rather, she dreamed of haunting him, of climbing unseen and unfelt into his single bed at night, of lying there on him and in him and by him while he gazed at the two-by-four-foot hole in his ceiling where the plaster had fallen down one night. He had woken with a start when it fell near the foot of the bed.

She leaned against the sink while he washed his face, then watched him stare into his own eyes in the mirror. Putting her face next to his, and staring where he stared, she could hear perfectly what he was thinking. It was, What's wrong with me?

When Luke and Beatrice left the bathroom, the phlebotomists were arriving. Luke continued back to the lab, but Beatrice stopped to watch them pass. Every morning she came up to watch the arrival. It was like a parade. They came down the hall in twos and threes, some with their arms around each other, some having recently left the same bed. Their names were Wendy, Elaine, Alan,

Randy, Eric, Arthur, Liu, Louisa, Amanda, Loric, Oliver, Nathan, and Elizabeth. Beatrice thought they were all very pretty, especially Oliver, who had a humongous head and beautiful pale skin that was always pink and vibrant-looking from the cold when he arrived. He looked to Beatrice like the sort of boy who drank great quantities of milk.

She liked to smell them, because each one wore a different cologne or perfume. Some days she spent her whole morning following them around as they slipped in and out of patients' rooms, drawing blood. But she would not do that today.

Today she waited patiently at the window and watched her friends as they finished up their work. She waited an hour before everyone was ready to go. It was customary for them all to go out to breakfast together. Otto suggested a pancake house. Everyone said that was a fine idea except Luke, who said he was too tired to eat, and started off down the hall. Beatrice did not follow him right away. She paused to watch her other friends walk off together in the opposite direction. She sent a prayer after them.

Let it happen this way, she said, gathering up her hair and waving it at them as if that might make what she wanted for them so. Let it be that Olivia and Otto encounter in each other something lovely, and Denis and Bonnie inspire each other's joy, and let something nice happen to Luke.

She knelt in an attitude of supplication and willed joy on her friends. In her mind's eye she could see the future as she desired it to be: Denis and Bonnie kissing in the bitter cold inside her car while they waited for the engine to warm; Otto and Olivia rubbing their feet together as they watched a movie in his apartment, and falling asleep with their heads touching and their breath on each other's faces. But for Luke she could imagine nothing.

Beatrice hurried after him, catching up as he was walking down the hill towards the river and the bus stop. The hospital grounds were beautifully landscaped, complete with a small wood that extended to the river. Snow was everywhere on the ground and trees, and still falling thinly. It was very cold. Luke had moved from Louisiana. He thought, on his way down the wooded hill, of his parents' house on Lake Pontchartrain. An ambulance wailed by him, going to pick someone up. He began to cry, but stopped by the time he reached the bus stop.

There was a girl there, huddled in a big coat, reading by the light of the streetlamps. She gave him a sullen look and turned back to her magazine. Luke sat down as far from her as he could. Beatrice sat next to him and considered trying to hold his hand. Luke closed his eyes and thought, for no reason he could think of, of the hole in his ceiling. He had still not cleaned up the plaster. He heard laughter.

Opening his eyes, he saw a woman coming towards him. She was dressed in a black shirt and white pants, and looked to him as if she had been out dancing. Her makeup was smeared on her face. He noticed, when she came near, that she reeked of booze.

"Excuse me," she said. "Pardon me." She was no one he knew.

"Yes," he said. He looked at her hair. It was all messy, but he could tell that it had at some recent time been elaborately styled.

"Can you help me?" she asked.

"I don't know," he said. There was little concern in his voice.

"I'm really bleeding," she said. "I just got my period, and I'm sort of without supplies. You know? Do you have any?"

"I think you should ask her," he said, indicating the reading girl with his head. The girl raised her head and looked at them briefly, then ignored them.

"I did. No luck. Have you got some tissues? A hankie? Anything?"

"Sorry," said Luke. He wanted her to go away.

"It's really bad," she said.

"I can't help you."

"Well," she said, touching her white pants, "am I spotting? Can you at least tell me that? I can't bend over enough to see. I think I'd fall. I'm not myself right now." Luke met her eyes for a moment. They were blue. He looked down at her crotch.

The woman burst out laughing. Nearby a man was laughing, too. Luke saw him step out of a shadow. The woman went to him. She put her arm around him, and they began to stagger off. Luke looked at the girl with the magazine. She was smiling. He stood up and moved his hands from his jacket pockets to his pants pockets, looking away from her. His face was hot. There was something in his pocket. He took it out.

It was the blue-topped tube that Denis had been missing. Luke had sworn he did not know where it was when Denis asked him, but now he remembered picking it up when Olivia forgot it on a counter. The blood in the tube was dark but not clotted. He held it in his bare hand. It was warm, from being next to his leg. With his thumb he worked the stopper free, then began to run after the woman and her friend. When he was close enough, he splattered it liberally over their necks and backs. The woman touched her hand to the back of her neck and brought it forward to look at it. When she saw the blood, she screamed loud enough to startle winter birds away from the telephone wires upon which they perched and sang.

"There!" Luke shouted. "There!" The man came forward and punched him square in the face. Luke fell down on the snowy sidewalk, where the man kicked him once in the head, then walked away with his friend, trying to console her. The magazine girl got up to wait for her bus at the next stop.

Beatrice sat down next to Luke. He was staring unblinking up into the dawning sky. He felt strangely content, lying there, and she was worried for him. She felt overcome by something. When she saw him falling back with blood spraying from his nose, love swelled in her like a sponge so she felt heavy for the first time since she'd awoken in the hospital. She reached out to him.

Though he could feel it when she stroked his forehead, he thought it was just a breeze. When she bent down and kissed him, he thought it was a twitch in his lip, possibly the result of brain damage from the kick to his head.

As she kissed him she had a vision of becoming his spirit wife. In time, she knew now, he would come to feel her and see her and know her. It would be as if she weren't even dead. The kiss itself, the contact, was thrilling. How could I have left this? she wondered, and she bent down to do it again.

But even as she kissed him, a sharp, clear note sounded in her head, and she knew with exquisite certainty that they had at last harvested her heart from her chest. It was on its way now to someone who needed it and wanted it. With her heart's disconnection, the veil obscuring her memory was lifted, and she recalled with perfect clarity the motivation for her leap. As the last quantities of blood drained from her heart, she stood up and threw out her arms, as if in benediction to the whole winter landscape.

Free at last! She cried, and ran off across the street and over the bridge. Halfway across she took off, went up and away, in search of a place without loneliness and desire; without rage, misery, and torture; without disappointment; without crushing, impenetrable sadness.

Listen, Leo

Listen, Leo, remember the lifeboat
we pilfered from what you said
was an abandoned garage sale,

1442 Columbus, not the explorer,
the street? Last night I came to,
retired to the basement to ponder

my position on circumspection,
the fate of the cruel & unusual,
& drink until I passed out.

I had my underwear on & my .45.
I was planning to feast on that bag
of Chicken Shack backs & beaks

we got at the place that went broke,
put my legs up on a six-pack & drift.
Anyway, this eerie glow started

emanating from the sewage pool,
mostly greenish. It winked
so I shot it, Leo, I've had enough!

Then this long low lump along
the wall near the bulkhead
started toward me, so slow

I had time to think. Went
to the attic & came back down
bearing Mr. Double-Aught.

Leo, I perforated the lifeboat.
It has become a dead one,
incapable, now, of surfacing

above its circumstance.
We can never return to it now.
It's gone. Gone like the snow.

Gone like I got a little behind.
It's a *sad* world, Leo, we fell,
like yesterday's laundry

into the tub, let's face a fact.
There's nobody left like us.
I got a weathered pate, you

got a ticket to Nova Scotia &
I'm swimming beside the boat.
When we gotta die, we're gone.

Leo, I confess, I adore your face.
Give me a little papa kiss.
Give me a muscle up. Leo,

there's nobody left like us.

for Steve Orlen

Nadezhda

When our reprieve began
I was reintroduced to Osip, my husband—
a gaunt man who walked
clutching his trousers. (Belts
could be used for suicide,
a serious offense.)

The prison staff was rosy-faced.
The young learn quickly: To kill
is good, to be killed, bad.

Soon they rise in the ranks,
have their photos taken
before a cardboard cutout
of a mountain.

We need a new Hogarth to depict
the official's progress, the prisoner's
(the first can become the second,
not vice versa).

As for Osip, he died
at 2nd River, a camp
on the way to a camp.

An Attempt

for Osip Mandelstam

For us, all that's left
is a dried bee, tilted
onto one wing.

Not long ago, a bloom
fastened its tongue, while its belly
tried unsuccessfully
to tip it backwards.

We mustn't touch—
anything without water
is without give.

This bee is our scout—
one day, dust
will pronounce itself
in the armatures
of every flower.
But we'll not be closer.

SUSAN BERLIN

Fat Crow Above Me

From a rain-stained square
tunneled into the rough-shingled
roof, the skylight begins,
in small creaks, to complain.

I crane, look straight up
at the bottoms of two black feet—
three prongs and inches, each;
between them dips the hammock
of a full-bellied crow, round and big
as the cauldron he belongs in.

From below, I see the point
of his blue-black beak as it pecks
at every speck of wet leaf left
from last night's epic squall.

Those legs—wires twisted to tripods
at the ends—imprints thrown across
my chest, the negative of his being
solid as sin on my body beneath,
and him framed, wholly, by heaven's blue.

SUSAN BERLIN

Still Life on Brick Steps

My brother and I without coats
on the front porch waved
goodbye, the day our father left,

with hands held low, close
to our chests, so our mother
behind us at the window

couldn't see. She stayed
inside, and when his car
took the corner, we turned

and saw her—the curtains,
long and white, parted by
her hands—her face

the face of a bride
abandoned too late, too
late, two lifetimes ago.

A '49 Merc

Someone dumped it here one night, locked
the wheel and watched it tumble into goldenrod and tansy,
ragweed grown over one door flung outward
in disgust. They did a good job, too: fenders split, windshield
veined with an intricate pattern of cracks
and fretwork. They felt, perhaps, a rare satisfaction
as the chassis crunched against rock and the rear window
buckled with its small view of the past. But the tires
are gone, and a shattered taillight shields a swarm
of hornets making home of the wreckage. How much
is enough? Years add up, placing one small burden on another
until the back yaws, shoulders slump. Whoever it was
just stood here as the hood plunged over and some branches snapped,
a smell of gasoline suffusing the air, reminding us
of the exact moment of capitulation when the life
we planned can no longer be pinpointed on any map
and the way we had of getting there knocks and rattles to a halt
above a dark ravine and we go off relieved—
no, happy to be rid of the weight of all that effort and desire.

ELENA KARINA BYRNE

Remote

How far, how far would it seem, ahead of the body?
Remote takes its time, taciturn.

Spool and furl, hope's quick unravel—remote:
a royal worth of dead watches. Replaced

hour, single shade, the white-put-there, polite winter,
strange chance. Remote turns pale and sends us away

to the next abstracted space where Remote's relatives live
in a remote village. Dreaming ahead of oneself.

Pace from refuge, irresistible: take the bright sting in love
remote cannot give because, distracted by nature, remote is remittent

and therefore not to be trusted. It cannot rage or chain-smoke
in the dark. These dull habits, careless words from our mouths,

with their indiscrete destination: Remote.
Political religion, riches, a simple way out.

There's the feeling of great loss in these things, what
can't be here, kept at arm's length.

By purpose, abandoned numbers know their argument
of the soul and the weakness in being alone. Remote. What

distance can surmount the small odds of two bodies in the world?
Insufficient as the burden thought: Remote, one, Remote, two.

What's Going On

Horses mosey across the black lake at the center of the sunflower.
I turn away when the pink sun sharpens its claws on the mountain.
Light blinks at the tips of leaves that suffer their sights underground.
Straw is beaming drumbeats back into stars.
The zippers of feathers are rejoining for flight.
Alone in a beer bubble a sweating violinist
links and undoes a chain of numbers.
Shells are building themselves in the sleep of seaweed.
It costs too much, so we don't pay attention.
A reindeer stag is rubbing moss off its headbranch,
a weapon whose incipience was pure imagination.
Matter imagines its future. This is how change happens:
desire becomes motion becomes texture in time.

VINCENT CIOFFI

Now I'm Building the World

First I place you in the garden
at the head of the white table;
fruit in a clay bowl,
flowers in their first opening
around you.

Now I build the wind,
one from the north
wreathed in cold
and from the south,
wet. I give you dominion
over wind.

Now I build the rooms
where I will love you.
In one I place the sea
and the sky, in another
the hills and the earth.
I paint the sky gray
and let the birds have it.
I give the hills your voice
and the shore your scent.

I get down on the ground
searching for one thing
that doesn't love you.
I elevate it over the earth
and call it God which,
in the language I am making,
will mean thing incapable of love.

Now I dig the grave,
a rectangle on the earth
three feet by seven feet.
I remove one hundred twenty-seven
cubic feet of dirt.
I fill it with myself
and what I have done for you.

SCOTT COFFEL

If I Must Be Saved

A spacious night, the ward quiet but for a male nurse humming
Klezmer music to your roommate, an elderly Polish
widow suffering in body only, her roofless
mind deluged by grace
as the first priest to orbit Earth
administers extreme unction to New York City,
its helium balloon of Christ punctured beyond repair
and dying in the orange and brown floodlights of Thanksgiving.

If I must be saved, let it be from the world to come.
Though it is wrong to twist silence into forgiveness
I'm tired of waiting for absolution.
If this is really you sleeping next to John's roses,
tell me quick why God fails the just and love dies—tell me quick
before this night slips westward against my will.

BILLY COLLINS

The Only Day in Existence

The early sun is so pale and shadowy,
I could be looking up at a ghost
in the shape of a window,
a tall, rectangular spirit
looking down at me in bed,
about to demand that I avenge
the murder of my father.
But the morning light is only the first line
in the play of this day—
the only day in existence—
the opening chord of its long song,
or think of what is permeating
the thin bedroom curtains

as the beginning of a lecture
I will listen to until it is dark,
a curious student in a V-neck sweater,
angled into the wooden chair of his life,
ready with notebook and a chewed-up pencil,
quiet as a goldfish in winter,
serious as a compass at sea,
eager to absorb whatever lesson
this damp, overcast Tuesday
has to teach me,
here in the spacious classroom of the world
with its long walls of glass,
its heavy, low-hung ceiling.

Tomes

There is a section in my library for death
and another for Irish history,
a few shelves for the poetry of China and Japan,
and in the center a row of imperturbable reference books,
the ones you can turn to anytime,
when the night is going wrong
or when the day is full of empty promise.

I have nothing against
the thin monograph, the odd query,
a note on the identity of Chekhov's dentist,
but what I prefer on days like these
is to get up from the couch,
pull down *The History of the World,*
and hold in my hands a book
containing nearly everything
and weighing no more than a sack of potatoes,
eleven pounds, I discovered one day when I placed it
on the black, iron scale
my mother used to keep in her kitchen,
the device on which she would place
a certain amount of flour,
a certain amount of fish.

Open flat on my lap
under a halo of lamplight,
a book like this always has a way
of soothing the nerves,
quieting the riotous surf of information
that foams around my waist
even though it never mentions
the silent labors of the poor,
the daydreams of grocers and tailors,
or the faces of men and women alone in single rooms—

even though it never mentions my mother,
now that I think of her again,
who only last year rolled off the edge of the earth
in her electric bed,
in her smooth pink nightgown
the bones of her fingers interlocked,
her sunken eyes staring upward
beyond all knowledge,
beyond the tiny figures of history,
some in uniform, some not,
marching onto the pages of this incredibly heavy book.

ROBERT DANBERG

Coconut in the Mail

for Mary

Sorry for the tardiness of my response.
I've been lost in thought, unable to reach you.
Your message arrived,
brown, brain-sized nut,
stripped to its rough shell,
my name and address singed on.
I want you to know I read it carefully,
held it to my ear and listened
to the mystery that sloshed within,
music of a lovely bathtub full of water.
I looked into it, great brown eye,
and thumped it like an M.D.,
heavy, oval heart in the palm of my hand.
It uttered syllables I know from inside my chest.
I fell in love with its journey from your hands to mine.
I want you to know it rests on the mantle
beside the iron my great-grandmother
dragged across the Atlantic in steerage.
It's taught me to sing close harmony.
It speaks to me of you, often.

Burning the Brush

I knew a force lay hidden in the air
that could raise this heat from only a spark,
lick the sky and still be hungry.
I lit a page of rolled up news and ran
out back with arm upraised and stuck
it under. It didn't catch at first.
I threw a cup of diesel on, and then another
and another, until a plume of smoke, blue
with rain, billowed up from the center.
A hemlock flared and crackled at the needles.
A birch burned down like a cigarette.
I stared at the fire that had formed a heart
and tongue together and raged in rain.
I watched it rise like a beautiful dress.
I imagined putting it on, a new garment
for this moment only put out by the next.
I'd wear it at death and submit
my soul as a body that burned like this.
I fell asleep open-eyed and dreamed of fire.
I heard a coal insist, *Spread this fashion*
of fiery dress across the land. Rise up
from here to your beloved. Burn forever.

Sugaring

You came down to me in the hollow after work.
I was reaping my just desert of overcommitting
myself this March to too many taps.
                              I was resting
for a while on a stump, listening to the steady
drip of sap in the pails.
                    You were dressed
in a skirt and purple blouse, whistling to find me.
I watched you descend through the trees like a goddess,
Diana's sister perhaps, whoever she was, the one
who lost her modesty.
                    I had ten more gallons to lug
up the hill.
            "You think each tree is a girl,"
you said.
          "The way they ooze from their holes.
The way they yield themselves."
                              "Yes and no,"
I said.
        "The way the first drop explodes
from the spout, followed by the second and third,
I thought of boys myself, but if you say girls..."

"It could be both," you said, "like Shiva."

I took you in my arms and held you like a tree,
slipped my hand beneath your skirt.
                              I was happy
in my confusion about which was which with regard
to the trees, knowing then as I held you in my palm
and studied the trees, that science is wrong
when left to itself.

I was seeing with both my eyes
that the world was one behind the guise of all
these leaves.
That the heart of my hand was deep
with darkness.

The Levirate

When it becomes possible to sleep with his brother's wife, George Norgaard jumps at the chance. He has in fact been wanting to sleep with her for years: he's spied on her at picnics, at Christmas, and once years ago they kissed too long—but nothing like this. Now they meet in hotels, in bars, at the Locks, and they are never seen. It is a safe affair. They are careful, and they handle it all with an aplomb that surprises him. His brother's wife is blond, with heavy hips. Her name is Marlene. She and George are both in their forties. George sees in her a lovely calm, unlike his own wife, a thin whippy woman he married very young. Not Marlene, who in bed is massive, and careful with him. If anything, he thinks, she seems a little bored. His brother in the Navy has cheated on Marlene for years in different cities around the world, and has come home to tell her all about it, and George, out drinking with his brother, has himself listened to a hundred stories. This one, that one. And now, George thinks, she is getting her own. His brother, he thinks, is a fool.

May is rainy that year, and there are constant storms. On the television news, houses tip precariously over ravines. The suburbs are flooded. A post office goes underwater, and downstream people pluck letters and packages from the trees. The news anchors are jolly, excited, and it pains George to watch. He is, he likes to think, a decent man. He wishes no ill on anyone, or hardly anyone, or so he often tells himself. Of course he doesn't. But in fact he is not entirely sure he is a decent man. Would a decent man do what he is doing? Probably not. But there are circumstances here. He could explain everything—he could—and, to himself, he does. Still, it worries him. Maybe, in fact, he is a bad man.

It's a rainy night in the hotel room when she pulls back the curtain. It's dark and windy, and they're very high up, and George can see forever, or so it feels: the black pool of Lake Washington, the red light on the university hospital, winking as it has done all his life. A man, he thinks, must climb up inside the light, now and then, and change the bulb. And the radio towers on Queen Anne, that job must be done, too. A thousand things to keep it all going. Everyone doing what is required. He himself is a fisherman most of the year, no harm in that. Most of his good fish go to Japan, past all the hills and out of sight, so he, too, is part of the larger world. George thinks of his brother in those foreign ports, eating that fish: it's possible, though not very likely.

They are in robes when a boy comes to the door with a tray. Bacon and eggs for her, a milkshake for him. George takes the tray and sets it on the desk, digs in his trousers for money, finds two dollars, and folds them neatly in half. "Here you are," George says.

"Just two bucks," says the boy, and disappears.

George closes the door after him. "Two dollars was enough," he says to the room.

Marlene begins to get dressed. "An unhappy boy," she says.

"For the love of mike," he says.

"Forget it," she says. "Honestly. Forget it."

"Okay," George says, "forgotten." He doesn't want to disturb her, not now. In a week he will be in Alaska, and already he is missing her. He'll be fishing for crab, high-walled seas looking huge the first few days, off the Chicagoff Islands and no help for hundreds of miles. But safe, if you know your limits, and George does. George, too, begins to get dressed. He picks up one of his long, ridiculous spotted socks.

The lamp flickers and goes out. George and Marlene look at it together, then out at the hills. Half-dressed, they say, together, "The storm." Outside, lights go out, block by block. It is a sight they will never forget. Sections of city winking out, up one side of a hill, down the other. George can hear the fuses blowing, the music stopping in the thousands of houses. People like themselves, half-dressed, looking up for a moment before understanding. All those faces turned upward. Then the scramble for the candles, the flashlights. Right now, he thinks, it's going on all over. Right there, he thinks, and picks a spot. It fills him with happiness. He and Marlene don't have to move, they are fine where they are: in the dark by the gusty window, with food. The city is dark now, dark entirely. The soft shapes of the hills are still apparent, the old shape of the earth. A moon comes out, scudding through the clouds. What measure of happiness do we deserve? he thinks. And then he thinks of the bellboy, caught in the elevator. "Ha, you fuck," he says aloud, gleefully, "you two-dollar shit fuck bastard."

Wizened

1. Other People

I begin with what I see plainly, before and around me. There is much to curtail. To one side, my neighbors are a family, extremely nuclear in a contemporary way. There's a mother, a father, a girl, and a boy, both children from previous marriages, the girl blond, the boy brunette, both juniors at the local private high school, both athletes (soccer). The kids, Jeff and Amie, own (that is, were given for Christmas) a basset hound named (by Jeff) Spliff, a word that his parents pretend they don't understand.

A good family: Mrs. Craven runs an antique store, and Mr. Craven is a corporate theft deterrent specialist. Amie plays clarinet, and Jeff's hair is longer than Amie's. Spliff runs in small circles and bays like a donkey, true to his breed. When Mr. Craven goes to another town to deter theft, Mrs. Craven goes along. She says they are taking the opportunity for a romantic getaway. She says instead of missing one another, they are making applesauce and lemonade, so to speak. The kids say, "Yeah, Mom, you just don't want him screwing around." Mom says, "That's me, I smother," and points at her cheek for a kiss.

I see it all though my sharp eyes, hear it all with my keen ears, and I'm mired with experience, dense with unfound wisdom. Mr. and Mrs. Craven pull out of the driveway, and soon, a dozen private high school kids, along with a dozen of their friends who were kicked out in seventh grade, and a dozen of *their* friends from public school, and a dozen of *their* friends who dropped out last year... dozens and dozens of kids arrive. I am the one who waits until the two-foot water pipe is pulled from under the bed and passed around, and then I am the one who calls the police. I am the bitch from hell, and what I need is a good fuck. I have nothing better to do, no business of my own to mind, and I don't shave. You can smell my bitterness, it's so old. When Mr. Craven does not have a business trip, I crouch in my car and wait for Amie and Jeff to sneak out their windows and hop into a van that waits up the block with its lights off. Then I follow the van to a neighboring development, and when the block is lined with cars and the house is filled with kids, I call the police on my cell phone, which I bought for this purpose and this purpose exclusively, since regardless of the fact that I am a *young* maid, and not an *old* maid, this is the business I mind.

I wait until the police have come, dispersed the children, and gone. Then I wait for the kids to gather at the golf course because it is not raining, and once they have set up their keg in a thicket, I call the police again. They must think I'm having a good giggle, but I'm serious, in a dead sort of way, because I have come to this, and, of all things, in this I believe. I know what happened to me. I became crotchety. En route to wisdom, I wizened. I terrorize with my morality. But I do take pleasure as well.

My neighbors to the other side are a homosexual couple about my age. They are graphic designers and work in a furnished garden shed in their backyard. In the morning, at eight o'clock, they walk out their front door with their briefcases, kiss like Europeans, and then one turns left and one turns right. Around their house they go, meet up at their shed, and shake hands. It's such a good, old joke to them that they don't have to laugh aloud for me to know how happy they are, how deep and ironic their ritual. When I go through my junk mail, I separate the good stuff, like "Herbal medicines enclosed" and "Check here for your free magazine." I peel away my address and leave the fat envelopes in their mailbox. When their Dalmatian bitch Goody digs a hole in the Cravens' yard, I fill it when no one is looking. I don't want a spat raging across my yard. I don't want the Cravens to have anything on the homosexuals.

Also, I experience compassion in my distanced way. Across the street lives a woman who is older than me, although no one knows it, because I have adopted the role I have adopted. I wear appropriate thick stockings and waistless housecoats. Vivian's husband left her a year ago, and so eager was he to travel around the world without her that he allowed her the house, makes the payments, and took with him only his credit cards, their daughter, their pet cockatoo, and, it is evident from my observations, his wife's will to survive. The bird died in the baggage compartment on a plane to Israel, but the girl, who is eight and has yet to speak a word, flies in from places like Crete and Bangladesh for monthly visits, collecting the exotic airline stickers on her suitcase. Various breeds of men hang around the house with Vivian, sometimes more than one at a time. They sit on her front porch in their boxer shorts. They play catch with the little girl in the dusk.

One at a time, each man's immoral afflictions are revealed to me. One man spent an afternoon in the yard, aiming a gun (not registered) at Goody, Spliff, and the front door of the homosexuals' house. One broke a bedroom window when he was trying to open it, then told Vivian it had always been that way. One slapped the little girl when she threw a ball and it hit his crotch. One refused to use a condom. One pocketed the change from Vivian's bedside table. It's the sneaks I can't stand. There are too many people in the world for me to allow for sneaks. That's how people get tangled up, sneaking around. If there weren't so many people, the sneaks wouldn't matter. They wouldn't tangle things up. The sneaks could sneak all by themselves. One of Vivian's men, though, a man with a willowy body and big, marble eyes, shot up heroin on my side of Vivian's hedges, under a streetlamp, at seven-thirty in the evening. I left him alone. I admired his gumption. The rest: I find out where they work and let their bosses know. I find out where they live and tell their wives. This, if not all things, is possible if you do your research and commit the time.

This is my sphere of influence. I have drawn a circle around the homes, making a fine subset for my purposes. In its center, I have drawn a circle around myself. I cover myself with clothes. Somewhere, I am inside the circles, inside my clothes, seeing with none but the relevant eye, the eye that sees within the context of my role, my worldview. Irrelevant eyes are elsewhere, living in the forms of sight I've rejected. Outside are the larger circles of the housing development, the earth, the orbits of other planets, and who knows what. If God appeared, He would be a circle.

When Spliff sneaks across my yard to have sex with Goody, I throw stones at him until he goes home, baying in circles. When Vivian's mute daughter falls from her bicycle, I set her on the porch, ring the bell, and run away. When Jeff and Amie ding the car, I spray-paint a circle around it, so it can't be missed. When the homosexuals begin to romance with the lights on, I close my shades so that they may have privacy, although, when I've had my nightcap already, I do allow myself to peek. Sometimes I spend the day making things for my house. I cut the bodice off an old sundress and make new curtains for the kitchen. I scrub the living room floor with sandpaper and paint it blue.

I am twenty-seven, and I have been crotchety for a good three years. I moved here when I felt it coming on. It began with a fear of other people's genitals. They are taking over the world. The fear filled me; a city of fear grew inside me, unarticulated, a mess of fear without unity, with outdated maps and such. I was, in fact, living in a city when I articulated the fear for the first time. It was all the people, trying desperately to organize themselves into box-shaped buildings but spilling into the streets, stepping all over each other, building and scrapping, and, worst of all, when they felt their humanity at its height, humanity in the form of lust or sentiment, extracting their sex organs and producing more of themselves.

When it comes to genitals and humanity, I give the homosexuals a break, because I think they have promise. But I do not give my parents a break, and I do not give myself a break, either. My parents have moved from this, my childhood home, to an identical house in another development, another cul-de-sac, another state. I think they had nothing to do without a mortgage. Three years, I've come to this and remained. My parents send me money because I hate them so much. I already tried thinking that it's time for something new to happen to me, for some new thought to take the place of my articulated fear. But I have already heard all the ideas. They're towered in the city of my fear. And I swear, I never get over it, the prospect of cleaner space, wider spheres, consequent mass widenings of individual existences. It gets me ga-ga, floats my boats, recharges my engines when I imagine it, so I work on my scheme for reduction, which comes down, plainly, to people. It's not the genitals as *such* that I mind, so much as the minds behind them, and what is done. A gun is not really a gun unless it's shot, you know.

It's along the lines of Jonathan Swift's idea on how to cure hunger using sick and starving children to feed folks. People thought he was serious, but then smarter people caught up with his irony. Smarter people still, like me, know exactly what was going on. The man knew he was right, and he knew the futility created by the condition of the biologic human heart. I mean, it was a good idea, and the problem is the old one where the heart says, in this case, "You can't kill *people*," and the mind says, "It sure would be good for those alive." So I work on my scheme, which involves the identification of pressure points on fault lines, the poisoning of potato chips, the introduction of ravenous, rabid animals to a metropolis or two, a grand network of anonymous assassins. I'm working it all out, rubbing my hands together with private glee, putting my self-doubt and grandiosity alternately into perspective, trying to construct a way to allow the remaining population a pure mourning, one that cannot blame, one that results, finally, in cleansing. This one, this idea, after many small ones, fills my mind. I cannot conceive of a better one, and I'm currently convinced it simply can't be done. The weaseling I do each day with the Cravens, with Vivian's men—the way I resort to the law of all things to clean my neighborhood—none would be necessary if I could finish the scheme. Not an easy job, but it keeps me going, and for now it keeps my great shakes in place.

But truly, I confess I am not stupid enough to believe I can do a thing to help people on such a scale, especially as I am no good at networking and hold no fascist claim to fame. So I keep the scheme to the sphere of my mind, because I haven't got it done, and because despite my best intentions, I am a good person, and can therefore be no more than an itch on a person's butt, a salve on a pimple, a bane to my own existence. I'm done examining why. It's so old hat, and it smells up a room.

ii. One Person

Which is not to say that I am always by myself, and which is not to say I never question the time I spend. For instance, merely months ago, someone knocked on my door. It's true, I ran upstairs, afraid that something had fallen from something, but I did, eventually, discover the cause of the banging, and interaction ensued.

It was a fellow, an up-front one as it turned out (I admire up-front), seventeen as it turned out. I invited him in, and he said, "Look, I'm not gonna dick around. Jeff next door, you know that kid, basically dared me to ask you out because he thinks I'll fuck anything." I considered. I straightened my stockings, which I wear even in the summer as part of my role, and asked him if he wanted tea. He said, "I drink coffee." I said, "Okay. I have some here somewhere." The fellow's name was Shannon, which as I remember can be difficult for a boy in school unless he is blessed with social acuity and popular acceptance, which this Shannon was. Good-looking in a contemporary way. Would make a pretty girl, but also played basketball.

It's true, I am wizened, sullen, frustrated, crotchety, but although the world generally annoys me, I have not lost interest in it. "What does Jeff want you to do?" I asked, hoping my smile was as wry as intended. Shannon scratched an ear and leaned against my kitchen table.

"He wasn't too clear, really," Shannon said. "Everyone knows what you're like. I guess old Jeff just said what he said. It's the kind of thing, if I was seven, I'd've knocked and run away, that kind of thing. He's laughing his ass off right now."

"I'm sure," I said.

I was still looking for coffee. Shannon walked around the room and then said he had to piss. I couldn't find any coffee, so I put water on to boil. Shannon came back.

"I'm gonna take off, I guess," he said.

"You're not going to ask me out?" I scratched an ear and leaned against my kitchen counter.

"How old are you?" he said.

"Thirty-five," I told him, settling for a balance between truths.

"Damn, girl. I'm in high school."

He considered. Then he said, "Okay, let's go out. I'll come over tonight."

"It's not like I'm eighty," I said, feeling excited by the prospect of, well, a prospect, I suppose. An inkling of kindness aimed at myself, I suppose, a lightness in my old bones.

So then he came over that night. I opened the door to him, and he said, "Let me in quick. I don't want everyone to see."

His hair was combed and wet. I'd taken my stockings off and dressed up the way I had in college when I went to the parties fraternities held at hotels. I'd looked at myself in the mirror for a while that afternoon, and in a girlish way, decided I would make a pretty boy. But by the time Shannon arrived, I'd almost forgotten my outfit, so busy had I been all evening, organizing my license plate file, which I use to keep track of people who speed on this road, and working on my scheme.

"You clean up good," Shannon said, and I thought he meant he liked my house, so I showed him around, and then something happened to me for a moment, something really kicked in, calm, even poignant as I remember, a softness he culled and leant me. Then we had sex on the blue floor in the living room.

And that's not all since I wizened: a couple years ago a friend of mine from college showed up on her way to visit someone else and borrowed my guest room for the night. She said it seemed I'd grown up a lot, which is what you say to someone who remains virtually silent for an entire visit, smiling in a wry way as you talk about a variety of things that are half-heard, old hat, and immediately forgotten.

Also, I wrote a letter to Ann Landers once, before I knew the scheme. Only half joking, I wrote, "Dear Ann Landers, I need some advice. So what should I do?" And I started a chain letter once, in an effort to solicit ideas. "Send me a good idea, a good idea to four more people, and so on. If the ideas are good we will all have good ideas!" Someone sent me a dollar, which is illegal, so I reported it, and that was that.

And my folks invited me for Thanksgiving, but I knew if I went I would seem to be giving solicitous thanks in exchange for food, which I believe is underhanded. So I let them know, by ignoring them, that I was still uncomfortable with their presence on the planet, and they sent me a check for fifty dollars.

So it's not like nothing ever happens to me. In fact, things continue to happen, which, it turns out, is a potential problem when it comes to settling on a way of life, or a continual sense of truth regarding one's ideology. For instance, I was supposed to have my period about two weeks after I met Shannon, but I didn't. I started jogging. I wanted my body to be strong in case I had to give birth. I went jogging with a pen and paper, so I could note the actions of sneaky people in the housing development sphere. I saw a man piss on his neighbor's lawn. I saw a pizza guy exit a house zipping his pants. I saw a girl drop an enormous vase from a second-story window. I wrote little notes, planning to place them in appropriate mailboxes, so that people would know what was going on. But then I suddenly felt like cutting up my flannel sheets and sewing them into layered squares to make diapers. And then I knew it was about time to check on the homosexuals; they had never disappointed me, never required correction, but I knew that if I wasn't vigilant, I could not be sure. And then I felt like cleaning out the guestroom and painting it yellow.

In short, I felt different. I thought about how I should adjust my scheme so that only the right people would die. I had never wanted the homosexuals to die because they were so nice, and I hadn't wanted Vivian to die, or her little girl, because they were so wounded, and of course, I admire wounds. I knew all this was my human weakness, and I tried, in my own way, to get over it. Trying to calm my human weakness was part of what I did when I worked on the scheme. With this new development, this lack of my period, a mere month ago, I began to find it so frustrating to work on my scheme that I cried a lot. I couldn't figure out how to sort through all those people.

It's hypocrisy I can't stand. It's how I'm always two steps from paradox, if not residing in it, if not allowing it to reside in me.

I cried so much that soon, I didn't think I was upset about the loss of an ideological structure. I admitted that the scheme could, after all, be one in a series of ideas. I thought, Something else *could* still occur to me and ring true, something different. After all, I am only twenty-seven. Some people don't get wizened until they're old. Some people don't at all. I wondered what I really meant by wizened. Did I mean bitter? Static? It is not necessary to think one thing and not another. It made sense, and felt good, to blame the tears on my newly churning hormones. It felt like something new, this unexpected lack of bleeding, a new something that I had never encountered, something of my own invention, that could not be thought up by anyone, or done by anyone else, a thing that had nothing to do with anyone else. This went on for a week or two. I felt light. I felt like a child. I felt full of potential, and it was great.

III. Another Person (Myself)

A long time ago, I guess it was before high school because I was still trying to find God, I was looking through my parents' desk.

They shared one. Her stuff was in the drawers on the left, and his in the drawers on the right. The surface was for bills only. I found my father's old cigarette roller, the kind with the handle you pull, and tried to make it roll various office supplies into Post-its, which didn't work out so well. Then I found a couple of chess pieces and some nail polish, so I painted faces on the chess pieces, which made them look downright demonic. Then I found my mother's collection of fortunes from Chinese restaurants, which were old, I knew, because my father hated and hates all that is Chinese. The fortunes said that her life was going to turn out in ways it had not, not then, not now, and they told her she possessed virtues I've never witnessed.

I found six photographs of our house, each taken from the same spot in our yard, right in front of the maple tree where I spent hours scribbling on a yellow legal pad. At the time, I was working on a novel. I'd been reading about Nazis, and asked my mother, "Who is our enemy now?" and Mother had said, "We don't have enemies anymore. The Russians, I guess." In my novel, a family would hear someone breaking into their house and whisper, "The Russians are coming!" and for pages and pages they would hide and plot and then emerge, trying to beat the Russians back with pitchforks and garden hoes, but the Russians would keep coming, so then the family got to live in the woods with kind animals.

In any case, the photos taken from in front of the maple tree preserved each color scheme in which the house had been painted—six colors already—the primaries, a couple secondaries, even Williamsburg Blue when that was the rage. All these colors, and I was still just a kid, though I felt older. It was as if someone wanted to keep track of what they'd done already, so they could check back, and see if they'd ever had it right. I remember thinking that they hadn't, and that I didn't even have a favorite. They hadn't ever had it right.

I found a sketch my father had made of my mother holding me as an infant, but he'd never gotten around to my head. I found a box of cherry stems, in brittle knots. Buttons never returned to shirts. Rusty paper clips. Single, double, and quadruple gummed staples that would never do a thing because anyone who can afford a stapler can afford new staples. Idiocy, everywhere. Idiocy just crammed into a decent-seeming piece of furniture, and I remember every item of it, every bit of hidden, accumulated, puerile waste. An inventory of other people's ideas.

That afternoon, when I forgot I was looking for God and examined the items at hand, that afternoon stretches when I think of it and holds years of weight. A small period of time can mean years in a person's life. A person knows only what a person knows, and time feels as big or small as it does according to how much space it takes up *now*, in a person's heart and mind. The time I have been living through in this house is permanent in this way, and this is why I can call myself, why I can be, why I *am* old. History is all bunched up behind me: what I know other people do and have done, all categorized, lumped, the facts of lives and occurrences undermined by failure, by the constant increase of trouble taking and having taken place, of lives documented, or forgotten, or both, or worse, remembered and useless. Useless? Failed? What on earth can I mean by that? I mean Vivian's men keep traipsing, the Craven kids are wallowing in banality, the homosexuals are shaking hands in their backyard. I mean, after a while, the pregnancy wore off. My period came back, innocent, saying, "Oops, I forgot, sorry," and instantly, that new feeling, the new idea, crushed itself into a minor moment, and I woke as from a nightmare.

I think there are too many people, and that's all I think. Still, looking from my little sphere with my relevant eye does not mean I'm without memory, or without imagination. For instance, I never liked Vivian's husband. I knew he would leave, or should, but I can see him, suited up for Safari, plainly and purely glowing, standing where giraffes knuckle over to drink, where tigers and zebras materialize from the grass as his past recedes. His little daughter holds his hand, and her first word is "Oh." At seven-thirty, the heroin addict steps off Vivian's porch and stands under the streetlamp until, at the end of the dusk, the light bursts on and he takes in his drug, linked, in his mind, with the stars. Vivian can see him from her window, and she allows him his pleasure, tacit, pretending for its sake that it doesn't exist. Her hair is long, full, and dark, her skin shining through the night-gown she has worn all day.

No one is left out when I watch my people. I can see Amie's subtle, appropriate sneer when she finds herself sleepless, watching the television sputter and chat. She makes tea, wanders the house and the yard. The night, the insomnia, is like years for her. She converses with it: she says, "I banish you, insomnia!" and walks it up and down the street. By morning she's collapsed on the couch, and when Jeff finds her he pulls an afghan over her body. He's a little confused, momentarily filled with a recognition of the vast spaces of which he's never conceived and never experienced. The day passes like wind. At dinner, their father breaks down at the table, half weeping, half laughing at the stock of his life. "I can't deter theft," he says. "It's too much. It's just everywhere." Mrs. Craven takes his plate of beans and potato and replaces it with berries in cream.

In the morning, the homosexuals lay a gingham tablecloth on the lawn and picnic for breakfast. They are dressed in their suits, but one stretches out and lays his head on his lover's lap. For hours, I think, his lover strokes his face from above. After a while Goody comes over, puts her head on the man's chest as he sleeps, and I think it's a family, whole.

A sphere, even if it is only one body wide, can be comfortable. Shannon gave me a good fuck, and I'm sure he will give many others, and better. He'll draw tenderness from the cluttered world and let it spill, making other people feel as I felt. The weight of the world can rise, history all fog and ghosts. I lift my eyes from the cul-de-sac and take a jaunt around my own place. Years ago, I threw a yard sale and relieved myself of the furniture my parents left behind, pieces too big and cumbersome in design or content to move. I look at what I brought to this house on my own, what space is taken or empty. I look at what I see and what I know. I think about war, how it can make a person feel half a unity, and I grow frigid with my fear. I repaint the guestroom a careful shade of neutral. I build a shelf in my kitchen and line it with empty jars.

In due course Mother and Dad Craven go out of town. Amie and Jeff throw a rockin' shindig. Kids come from all over the county, and the cops hang up when I call. They recognize my voice.

Vivian slaps the shit out of her little daughter for walking in on her and the heroin addict. The girl, dumb in this country, finds the addict's stash and mixes it with roach poison.

Spliff sneaks up on Goody, and one night Goody lays a litter of spotty, baying puppies. The homosexuals creep into their backyard in the dark, dig a hole, take one puppy at a time by the hind legs, and slam it against the wall of their garden office, drop each into the hole, and cover it up.

I am old, after all, and plenty dead. I've barely begun to work out the angles in my scheme, ridden as it is, still, with sloppy thinking, hypocrisy, and logistic impracticalities. As it is, with nothing new, there is too much work to be done.

An Interview with Stephen Dobyns

Stephen Dobyns is the author of nine books of poetry, including *Concurring Beasts, Griffon, The Balthus Poems, Cemetery Nights, Body Traffic, Velocities,* and *Common Carnage.* He is also the author of a collection of essays on poetry, *Best Words, Best Order,* and nineteen novels, ten of which comprise a very popular series of detective books, known as the Charlie Bradshaw mysteries, set in Saratoga Springs, New York. He began his writing career as a police reporter in Detroit.

LAURE-ANNE BOSSELAAR: In his book of essays, *Orphan Factory,* Charles Simic ends one of his essays by saying: "It makes absolutely no difference whether gods and devils exist or not; the secret ambition of every true poem is to ask about them, even as it acknowledges their absence." What do you think about that?

STEPHEN DOBYNS: Well, I think you're always asking about them. One of the functions of poetry is to create a cosmology, to map out the dimensions of what we imagine reality to be, and what, then, may be beyond that. We're always dealing with our existential isolation and trying to decrease that isolation. So that by mapping out that greater area, there's always the attempt to people it. And when one tries to people it with something larger than human, some kind of spiritual or deific creature, then one's not only peopling it, but attempting to create a reason for being as well. It becomes part of our constant endeavor, identifying the reason for populating a cosmos. That's one of the reasons one writes. But the basic reason is to try to erase the isolation.

BOSSELAAR: Camus once told his students: "Writing is a man's trade, *not* God-given inspiration." In a recent interview in *The Connecticut Review,* Richard Eberhard said: "I believe in inspiration, which is not a popular concept these days." In your essay "Writing the Reader's Life," you say: "The act of inspiration is, I think, the sudden apprehension or grasping of metaphor." Can you extrapolate about that?

DOBYNS: Any piece of writing is a metaphor which, at one level, stands for or represents the writer's relation to what he or she imagines the world to be. By relation I mean emotional, spiritual, intellectual, physical. So you hit upon something that you can use as metaphor; for instance, a liar is like an egg in midair—that metaphor that W. S. Merwin uses. To hit upon the idea of the egg in midair may lead to the realization that one can use this to present an idea of the liar, what it is to lie. All art is metaphor. Even Anna Karenina obviously is metaphor. So as I say, that aspect of intuition is to hit upon something that will function as metaphor. But it may not be an idea, it may be a sound or it may be just a wriggling in the brain. One writes something to find out why one's writing it, and one pursues it. And in that search, often the metaphor evolves. I don't believe in inspiration as something that comes from the other. I think all that comes from within the self. But there are different aspects of the self, the conscious self and unconscious self. Sometimes that act of inspiration seems to be a joining of that conscious and unconscious self. There's suddenly a kind of traffic between those two places, because the metaphor that one suddenly understands has to have some kind of psychological relation to the person who's having it. It's not an arbitrary grasping. It's something with some personal, psychological, spiritual, emotional meaning.

BOSSELAAR: Right, right—but then art is the *consequence* of grasping the metaphor. It is the discovery of how and why one has grasped that metaphor.

DOBYNS: In part. I mean, art becomes something made. And what makes it art is the nature of that end product—that there is something within it which corresponds to our definition of art.

BOSSELAAR: I know that music has a very big importance in your life, and that you like many kinds of music: classical, jazz, rock-and-roll. You often listen to music when you write. How does it help your writing?

DOBYNS: It orders the silence, it orders the chaos. I don't write all the time to music, but sometimes I do. And otherwise, it's often playing. And it can be mixtures, as you say, of classical or jazz or South American. I don't listen to that much rock-and-roll anymore; I find the lyrics too tiresome. I also listen to music for the rhythms, that there is much in the rhythms that I try and use in the poems. So there's also that aspect of listening in order to steal, if I hear something that I think works well, or that I might be able to use. And I'm sure that in some ways I use it for completely middlebrow reasons, almost as Muzak. But beyond that there's that general sense that it orders the silence around me. It gives structure to it. And it gives me a constant example of art, of a kind of metaphor which is being presented through the medium of sound.

BOSSELAAR: Which brings me to noise. In our many conversations about poetry, you often mention liking the noise in certain poems. What exactly do you mean by noise?

DOBYNS: Most simply, it's rhythm; and then on top of the rhythm there's the relationship between stressed and unstressed syllables; and on top of that there's the sound of different consonants, the relationships between different consonants; and then beyond that there's the relationship of vowels; beyond that there's the relationship of pitch. And so you have those different aspects of sound, which you try and weave into some kind of a pattern, something which may not even seem to be a pattern. But often the poem will begin with a particular sound that works as a kind of tonic note that I keep up through the poem, and sometimes I'll switch to another pattern, or sometimes keep the same pattern all the way through, which can be no more but a simple *t* sound. The noise aspect of it becomes one of the things that I like best about it. And also that the noise can have some metaphoric relation to the content, and can point to a greater kind of cacophony in the world, a greater kind of chaos in the world, so that while the content can be fairly mellow, the noise in the background can be the opposite, can seem nearly out of control. That becomes something else that I like: the sense of the poem in its noise as being almost out of control, seeming to be out of control, yet never out of control.

BOSSELAAR: What directed, what influenced the noise in "Freight Cars"? I hear it in the first two lines: "Once, taking a train into Chicago / from the west I saw a message / scrawled on a wall in the railway yard." There's an emphasis on the assonances.

DOBYNS: Well, the first noise is the "Once/west" rhyme, and then using as you say the "wall," all those noises: "scrawl," "rail." In the making of the poem was the desire to create a series of noises, relationships between those noises, that would have some metaphoric relation to the subject matter, and which would be almost cacophonous, in that what the poem then deals with is the lost, a world populated by people who are wandering and wandering. And that all our rationalizations, all our statements of what we're doing and what we're worth and what we're meaning to do, etc., etc., are just so many bits of color imposed on that basic idea of wandering, wandering. And what becomes most important obviously in the poem is the relationships between people, and that those relationships become sacrificed to these ideas of ambition or desire or—

BOSSELAAR: [Quoting a line in "Freight Cars."] "Imagining some destination for oneself..."

DOBYNS: Exactly. [Quoting another line.] "Some place to make all the rest all right."

BOSSELAAR: Yeats, who I know you admire, once said: "Great art chills us at first by its coldness, or its strangeness, by what seems capricious; and yet it is from these qualities it has authority, as though it had fed on locusts and wild honey." I love that quote, and find it particularly appropriate to your poetry. Who for you wrote or writes "great art" today? In fiction or poetry? And could you briefly explain why those authors are important to your work?

DOBYNS: I don't know if anyone alive now writes great art. I expect that they do; I don't have the objectivity to judge it or to look at it that way. I was struck the other night listening to C. K. Williams read how marvelous those poems were, and how completely they made a shape—his poem "Ice," for instance. There are people that I like: Thomas Lux's poems, I admire greatly; Simic's poems, I admire, and some of Mary Oliver; Ellen Bryant Voigt, Louise Glück, and a few others. But when I think of that quote and who it brings to mind, it has to be people like Rilke. Perhaps Baudelaire, perhaps Neruda. But Rilke comes closest to personifying those words for me. Given the strength of that remark by Yeats, I think, Who is this true of? There are a few Yeats poems, there are a few of Philip Larkin's poems, a couple of Auden poems...I can't think of any Lowell poems, I can't think of anyone in those other generations. There are certainly poems that I love by Roethke and Berryman and Lowell and Bishop, but none that do that kind of work on my interior, as is suggested by that quote. That's something that I see in Rilke more than anyone else.

BOSSELAAR: And in fiction? Chekhov?

DOBYNS: I suppose Chekhov. I admire him certainly more than anyone else. Possibly some Faulkner, but I'm not even sure of that. A book I read recently that I felt was powerful in that way was Thomas Mann's *Doctor Faustus*. It had that kind of strength. Other writers that I like—Kundera, I think is a marvelous writer. Also Cormac McCarthy, also William Trevor. But of those three, William Trevor is the one that I admire the most... what he's able to do. Yes. I don't know if there's anyone in poetry who can do anything comparable to what Trevor can do in prose.

BOSSELAAR: Often, when I ask you what poetry you're reading, you're reading either South American or East European poets. You seem to prefer them to many contemporary American poets. Why?

DOBYNS: I really despise American popular culture, and so its appearance in contemporary fiction or poetry becomes sufficient reason for me not to read it. It's one of the reasons I also don't see many American films. It seems to be a culture driven by a frenzy of appetite, that has no empathy, no sympathy, no roots, no direction. It's just a matter of filling its belly as quickly as possible. There's other kinds of writing—I mean, I used to read mystery novels, Chandler and Simenon. There are the high peaks that one reads for and then there are the low peaks that one reads for, and obviously there are far more low peaks than high peaks. But Thomas Mann's novels, certainly, I would see as high peaks. Dostoyevsky, all the Russians, seemingly. Otherwise I can't think of any contemporaries except for the ones I've mentioned. And the Poles, there are five or six great postwar Polish poets, beginning with Zbigniew Herbert.

BOSSELAAR: To go back to your own poems, and to the "sudden apprehension or grasping of metaphor"—what sudden apprehension or grasping of metaphor occurred when you wrote a poem as wild as "The General and the Tango Singer" in *Cemetery Nights,* or more importantly the Cézanne sonnets in *Body Traffic*?

DOBYNS: "The General and the Tango Singer" is for me much more of a political poem, with these two definitions of art being argued at the expense of the world around them. What is going to triumph in the world? Is it going to be this definition of art or that definition of art? Well, basically, by that kind of ignorance what will triumph in the world is the fire which obviously destroys the restaurant and will destroy other things as well. That is one of the poems that I wrote when I was living in Santiago, Chile, and it was certainly affected by living under a dictatorship, with a curfew, with constant evidence of living in a police state. That's what the General represents, that aspect of it. As for the Cézanne sonnets, I think more and more I was seeing Cézanne as someone who I wished I could emulate. I don't mean necessarily in his ability or his skill, but his concentration on the work to the exclusion of all else. It would seem that he had every reason to stop painting, because he was surrounded by people who told him how bad it was, from all the critics who were writing, from many contemporary painters of his time, from his best friend, Zola, from his wife and son—everyone. And he was very crude, his table manners were awful, he was clumsy in his speech, he was very shy, yet he continued to work, with a single-mindedness that really approached madness, considering how determined it was. And even the fact that he died in the midst of working. He was working on one of those last landscapes, and it rained. He was in his sixties, he caught cold, and was dead three days later. He'd stayed out in the rain trying to finish what he was doing. I admired that steady-mindedness in the face of all else. The world becomes a tremendous distraction. It's hard not to pay attention to it, to be caught up in ideas of success, ideas of publication, ideas that people are patting one's head. "People like my poems, they don't like my poems," or bullshit like that. Ideally I should just have the poems themselves, as Cézanne seemed to have the painting. I'm not saying that would result in better poems—there clearly have been poets, painters, and musicians who have worked with that same steadiness of purpose whose work never amount-ed to anything at all. What I admire is that ability to work with-out interruption.

BOSSELAAR: And is the sonnet form of the Cézanne poems appearing in groups throughout *Body Traffic* a kind of willed structure and homage? A metaphor within the metaphor?

DOBYNS: Just to the degree of linking it to the history of art, of linking it to the tradition, that art is something ongoing, that has a past, a present, and ideally will have a future; to write those poems in an established form, yet also taking liberties with that form.

BOSSELAAR: Which you did.

DOBYNS: It seemed to make the homage more significant to me.

BOSSELAAR: About discipline: do you have a strict writing discipline? When do you write the poems, when do you write fiction, or journalism, or the mystery novels? How do you go from one to the other?

DOBYNS: It goes back and forth—if I'm caught up in an idea for a poem or for a series of poems then I work on those, and the fiction gets pushed off a little bit. When I'm busily revising the poems, then I'm also able to work on the fiction. When I finish a larger novel, then I'll often do a mystery novel right after that. The fiction creates an order in my life that I find useful. If I only wrote poems, then I feel my life would be far more disorderly. But the practice of fiction requires a plan, it requires doing something every morning, working on it every day, maintaining that schedule, following an outline. And that makes my life more orderly than it might otherwise be. If I could write poems far more at will and have it come at any time, then I suppose I would do more of that and less of the fiction. But I also write fiction for economic reasons: it pays the bills. And I have very mixed feelings about that, really. I sometimes wonder what kind of writing I would do if I didn't need that money. It's a distraction rather than a burden. I love writing fiction as well.

BOSSELAAR: When will your next book of poetry come out? What is its title?

DOBYNS: The next book's scheduled to come out from Penguin in the fall of '99, and it's called *Pallbearers Envying the One Who Rides*. It's a group of sixty poems which is split in the middle by a long other poem called "Oh, Immobility, Death's Vast Associate." The sixty poems are all about one character, who I call Heart. Ideally, one learns how to read the poems, and so the first thirty poems show one how to read the later poems, which are far more complex in their arguments, in their meditations, in their language, in their syntax, in their sound. I suppose to some degree we don't see the character from early life until late in life, but the development of that character follows some kind of chronology. The poems that conclude the book are more concerned with the end of life, and the poems that begin the book are more concerned with those emotional relationships which we value in the middle of our lives.

BOSSELAAR: Who is Heart? You?

DOBYNS: Heart is not me. He's not a persona for me. He has many childlike and absurd aspects—in that way, he's closer to the [Christian] Morgenstern poems, which are poems that I've read for a long time, and which were one of the influences for the series. He's also somewhat like Henry, but Henry's far more sophisticated in the Berryman poems. As is Mr. Cogito, far more sophisticated in the [Zbigniew] Herbert poems. So they're closer to the Morgenstern, although Morgenstern's poems are mostly comic. These poems of mine often use the comic to move to a much more serious conclusion.

BOSSELAAR: To go back to the body of your poetry: in *Concurring Beasts* you were very much influenced by, or aware of, the Vietnam War and the Democratic Convention in Chicago. When you wrote *Griffon* you were a journalist for *The Detroit News*—so again, one feels the influence of the outside world. Some poems in *Body Traffic,* the new poems in *Velocities,* and some poems in *Common Carnage* have to do with Chile. There is a political attentiveness present, but not constantly so, in your work. Some of your books have no autobiographical poems—like *The Balthus Poems,* for example. In *Body Traffic* one feels you are completely engaged with the autobiographical. I feel this movement of looking out, looking in, looking out. Is that willed?

DOBYNS: All my poems are autobiographical; all my poems are political. Sometimes they're more obviously autobiographical, and use the first-person pronoun. Anything I write about—if I write about a chair, and talk about nothing but the chair—I'm still writing an autobiographical poem. There's just no way for a human being to not do that. At the same time, if I'm writing about an event which I believe happened, then there's no way that I can write precisely or realistically or truly about that event. All autobiography really becomes a form of fiction, because I'm seeing it through a filter that's so subjective that its relation to what actually happened may be impossibly distant. As for the political, there's always that question behind every work of art: how does one live? Sometimes that's focused very clearly on the events within the society, and sometimes it's more internalized. But the very nature of that question—how does one live?—obviously has its political dimension. So those become constant concerns. One of the attempts of art, ironically, is to use the subjective to try and be free of the subjective, to break loose of the self by using something which is totally of the self. In dealing with the question of how does one live, one is attempting to grasp some larger sense of the political, some larger sense of the society, and be able to identify oneself as a participant, as a member within that society. That becomes very tenuous, especially if you're arguing from a position of existential isolation, where you're wondering, Do I really exist at all? To what degree am I a figment even to myself?

But I have pretty much the same themes all through my books, and basically from one book to another, I'm choosing to deal with those themes slightly differently; I feel that I've found a new access, or a new way of writing about those themes, or I feel that my command of the language has become more precise. All of it, I think, is trying to get through the mirror to the other side, to the so-called real. And that just may be a case of self-delusion. Yeats says that we write about the same themes all our lives. When I first read that in his autobiography at the age of twenty-two, it seemed preposterous. Now at fifty-seven, I think it's true. And I could find poems that I've written again and again and again. They may be similarities that nobody else would recognize, but they're recognizable to me. One seeks paradigms, new ways of doing something, and when a paradigm is discovered, then usually that can result in a new body of poems. It may be that that body of poems constitutes a whole book. In this new book, *Pallbearers Envying the One Who Rides*, that whole book is controlled by the new paradigm. That was also I think true of *Cemetery Nights* and *Body Traffic*. That can be very exciting, because you feel that you have this huge thing in front of you and you're trying to map out all its dimensions. And the writing of the poem is the mapping of those dimensions. And you do it until every scrap is gone. Then it's over, and you sit there half out of breath and half impatient for some new paradigms to take its place.

BOSSELAAR: How important is friendship for you?

DOBYNS: I find it the thing that really sustains—yet I suspect that I also have great doubts about it. One has been betrayed in one's life, or has betrayed others, and so one sees the fragility of friendship. Yet if the enemy is really existential isolation, if the enemy is the solipsistic, then friendship is one of the only tools, or one of the strongest tools one has to defeat that enemy, and so it has to be constantly nurtured.

BOSSELAAR: But isn't there also the constant fear of losing that friendship? And the temptation of preferring isolation to the pain of that loss—be it through death or disloyalty?

DOBYNS: I think that's a danger. The people I know who have chosen to be single, who have chosen to have not friends but acquaintances, all veer into eccentricity, and are unable to judge themselves accurately. They're unable to judge their work, they're unable to judge the right and wrong of any situation in their lives. It's not simply a matter of becoming self-indulgent. They no longer are able to see themselves in relation to the world. We need friendships for many things, but one of the reasons we need friendships is to keep us sane, because without them we veer off.

BOSSELAAR: But when a dear friend dies—an *essential* friend, someone who has been integral to your life like your friend the Spanish painter José Berruezo—what happens then?

DOBYNS: Then there's a great vacancy in one's life. One's reaction to any death is partly a selfish reaction: How can this person have deserted me? How can this person have removed himself or herself from my life? Didn't they know I needed them? That's very difficult. I think the tendency then is to close down, and not let any person get that close. But that's even more destructive. One has to remain vulnerable to pain. If you're going to be an artist, you have to remain vulnerable to pain. If you become completely self-sufficient, completely impervious, then you can't make anything that anyone's going to ever care about. [Long silence.] I mean, all that you're finally left with is wit.

BOSSELAAR: Yes . . . and books. But they don't talk back.

DOBYNS: No. They don't talk back.

Like a Revolving Door

Heart feels sad. He's tired of being a heart
and wants to be a lung. A lung never lacks
a sister or brother. He wants to be a finger.
A finger always has a family. Or a spleen
which only feels anger and is never sad.
Sometimes Heart feels joyous, beats with vigor.
But then the old stories resurface again:
hardship, cruelty, the Human Condition.
A kidney never faces these problems alone.
The eyes in unison devise a third dimension.
Not by being solo do the ears create stereo.
But Heart must turn outward for comradeship,
to seek another heart, a journey fraught
with uncertainty. Like a revolving door—
such is falling in and out of love. And
the betrayals! Heart needs only to consult
his book of broken hearts to feel pessimistic.
But soon he puts on a fresh shirt and heads out
to the highway. He hangs a red valentine heart
from a stick so people will guess his business.
No matter that the sun is sinking and storm
clouds thicken. Approaching headlights glisten
on his newly pressed white shirt and on his smile
which looks a trifle forced. Dust catches in his hair
and makes him cough. Why is Heart alone in the chest?
Because hope is an aspect of the single condition
and without hope, why move our feet? To see himself
as purely a fragment: such is Heart's obligation.
Let's swiftly depart before we learn what happens.
Sometimes a car stops. Sometimes there is nothing.

74

Thus He Endured

Heart's friend Greasy got nixed by a stroke.
His pals give him a wake; they drink all night.
The next day they cart the coffin to the church.
In life, Greasy waxed cars; now he's defunct.
The priest says how Greasy's in a better place.
Heart takes exception. What could beat this?
Some mourners weep; some scratch their butts.
In life, Greasy was a practical joker. Even salt
in the sugar bowl wasn't too trifling for him.
When the service is over, Heart and five others
heave the coffin on top of their shoulders.
Outside it's raining. They wait for the hearse.
Maybe it's late, maybe it showed up and left.
The priest locks the church. Cars drive away.
Let's carry the coffin, it's just a few blocks.
They set off. Heart hears a whistle. Show some
respect, he gripes to one of his buddies in back.
In life, Greasy often asked, What's the point?
and What comes next? Heart thought his jokes
helped keep the dark at arm's length. Rain drips
down the pallbearers' necks. Because of the fog
they can't see beyond their noses. Right or left?
If their hands weren't full, they would flip a coin.
Someone plays the harmonica, then starts to sing.
The pallbearers look at each other, it's none of them.
In life, Greasy reached three score and ten.
He had a wife, three sons, and five Great Danes
but not at the same time. He always drove a Ford.
Did we take a wrong turn? asks Heart. The rain
turns to sleet; it's getting dark. Someone starts
playing the trombone. A tune both melancholy
and upbeat. Where could it be coming from?
In life, Greasy felt a lack. He worked too hard,
the holidays were short. His wife kept asking
why he didn't do better. Then his sons left home.

Greasy stuck rubber dog messes on the hoods
of all his pals' cars. This is what life's all about,
he'd think. Thus he endured. It begins to snow.
Heart shoulders his load. The snow goes down.
Will Greasy get planted today? Guess not. Heart
stares at his feet. He can't see that the coffin lid
is tilted up and Greasy perches on top just a shadow
of his former self. With both hands he flings wads
of confetti. He's a skeleton already. Heart would
scratch his head but he'd hate to let his corner drop,
his pals ditto: pallbearers envying the one who rides.

SHERRY FAIRCHOK

Holding the Mare

When we undressed in the tack room, we kept our backs turned,
cradled our new breasts like the barn cat's kittens
and counted ribbons strung like tiny laundry overhead:
blue, red, yellow, white, pink, green. We giggled in the dark there
over the school nurse's diagram, the new words.
But we all said yes, as if we'd done it before,
when the riding instructor asked us to hold a mare to be bred.
We knew about mares coming into heat, all pinned ears and
     hoof-stamp
when we brushed against their rumps, and we'd watched
the thick eel of a gelding's penis descend, its downpour
glossing over cobblestones we'd just swept clean.
We said yes. And then Suzanne quieted
the mare's head while Sarah bent at her flank, cupped
a back hoof to keep her from kicking. A flick
from her long tail nicked my eye to tears.
I was supposed to lift it, bare the gray suede pucker of her sex
when the approaching stallion reared up
his erection rapping the air like a blind man's cane—
but as his haunches punched hard into her rump
the tailbone burned through my hands like a rope.
I let go and the penis popped out.
"Guide him, guide him!" our teacher cried.
The pale root waggled at my right hand, more willful
than the small horse whose ears I'd scratched
when shedding made him itch. I had to know:
Would it feel rubbery, or soft as his nose?
My fingers clasped it as the teacher's fist closed
above mine, shoving it into its pocket, quick as shoplifters,
and we both stood back, triumphant, as if we'd matched

77

a jigsaw piece with its gap, and our picture was complete.
Outside the barn, waiting for our mothers' cars,
Sarah asked me, "What did it feel like?"
and both girls stared at my palm, and I knew
all night I'd remember, and in the morning
still have no words for it.

ROBERT FANNING

Making Sure the Tractor Works

A drunk man reels his tractor around
the square lawn, midnight. His wife stares
from the front door window as if
on a half-sunk ship's deck at a shark

tearing through the dark water. She chews
her thumbnail raw. Two of their sons, in blue
pajamas, shuffle across the linoleum
rubbing their eyes. She plays the bear

again, gets them to giggle by growling,
by chasing them upstairs to bed. She tucks
them in, strokes their hair, the air thick
with model train glue, sneakers, and fear.

The tractor, roaring, rumbles under the window.
*Dad works very hard, boys. He's just
making sure the tractor works, now go to sleep.*
She blesses their foreheads, leaves the door

open a crack, and disappears. Down the hall
her voice spills into the phone.
The older boy buries his head
under his pillow as his brother climbs in.

Dad's grinding orbit rattles close,
then off around the house. Rattles close,
then off around the house. His headlights
wobble onto their wall as he bounces over the lawn,

the driveway, the flower bed, the sandbox.
Shadows of tree branches drag across
their trophies and team photos, down
their closet door and away. When sunlight

breaks their windowpane, they wake late
for school and dress with no words. The bus
thunders past their house. They stare at soggy stars
and moons floating in their cereal bowls.

Outside, in her nightgown, their mother
stumbles over the rutted lawn barefoot,
pressing clumps of sod back down.
She chucks into a bag the evidence,

in scattered pieces, of last night:
a shredded mitt, a mangled plastic bat,
a headless action hero. She backs the tractor
into the shed, stashes the keys.

She stands upright: the birdbath, the statue
of Mary from the crushed rose bed—prays
to herself, then turns toward the house,
toward whatever else she can still repair.

The Amphibrach

(Amphibrachys pedalis)

This rare symmetric
newt has short limbs that abut
a strong unspotted body.

Its habitats are worldwide,
but naturalists list it as native
to Limerick.

Hatched from equipoised egg,
the newborn amphibrach swims
to rhythms of water

rippling in rural ponds;
wriggles equal forelimbs to dodge
the gape of fish-mouths.

As tail flutters to a stump,
fickle gills gasp in water, it
crawls into dry worlds,

looks evenly left and right,
fore and aft, its tongue alert
for two satisfying bugs.

How does it cope with copulation?
By holding a startled mate at both
balanced arms' length?

Waking

Surfacing from the deepest pool
I've ever fallen into, I emerge
gasping for air, and searching
for something to tell me
where I am and how I got there.

Strangers dressed in white
who aren't nice don't tell me
anything I need to know.
They just circle the bed, brandishing
that tube that brings a choke to my throat.

I can't understand why I don't eat
food or drink water. In my mind
conspiracy collaborates with cruelty
to confuse me. I don't think they know
I'm awake, so I close my eyes tight.

When's morning, when's night?
Where's the sun and all the people?
I can't talk and no one speaks to me.
My hand finds the plastic tube up my nose
and I pull its bloody length from me.

Suddenly I'm crying and asking
for my mother. No one understands me,
so I flop around in my bed
like a caught fish on an arid beach,
then, my mother's smiling face.

I can't ask why, where, or what,
but I do know when; it's now,
my new birthday, as I push free from
the coma-womb, and I'm aware
that this second birth leads to a new life.

New life, second chance to get things
wrong or right. I have a lifetime
to recognize my own voice,
an opportunity to relearn
everything from my seated position.

MICHAEL FITZGERALD

Ballot

for Jeanie Bauserman

This year, I vote
for the ash and linden trees,
the boxwood shrubs, the magnolia,
the blacksmith, the curator,
the music of motherhood,
I vote for the pylons of fathers,
the man in the turban,
the sitar player,
the Nigerian drummer,
a country walk, a walking mall
in the center of town,
the orchestra players,
the Javanese gamelan players,
I vote for bicycles, literacy,
the house husband,
the Native American flute players,
thousands of service works, each one
pinned to their pay.

RICHARD P. GABRIEL

Jimmy, Jimmy, Oh Jimmy Mack

—James Michael Maguire, 1953–1980

Jimmy's grave is flat and nothing
in the cemetery grove of fat maples
blowing electric green not a mile from the river
wind blowing like the background sound
of highspeed tires on the highway not far away
nearby toy trucks and a two-month-old's grave
playing dead but it's Jimmy I found
curled black Jimmy in his box
whose head thrown through sheetrock
was a missile aimed at his mother's cunt bursting out black Jimmy's
voice knocked from his head Jimmy bare
in the trees by the stone wall we tried
being girls by the side of the road we lay
on each other and he whispered lust my name
and Buddy and Jimmy and me with the girls
in the sandpit Buddy a man
almost and Jimmy and Buddy bare jumping from the sand cliffs
for the girls to watch Buddy hard
and I told them it's OK it's OK
but they hunched in a circle thinking God Jimmy
in a school for the deaf for imbeciles coming home
Jimmy in the shootout
with cops in his car to escape his head
through the windshield the oak
bark the meat through the other side
past the sandpit the highway the river Jimmy
laughing Jimmy
whose voice was bunched on one side of his head the cracks in his skull
like the hammer in her cunt Jimmy
under ground his stone flat and nothing only the baby
can laugh under ground in his box full of toys
in the electric green cemetery by the river wind

85

blowing the sand over grass with my eyes with no cracks
in my head to see with
no cracks in my head
direct to you
Jimmy

Leaf of My Puzzled Desire

A leaf falls in high wind and drifts
along a path unfolding by simple rules:
rise away from heat, sink toward cold.
I'll claim this mirage
forming in the heat field tinged
the reluctant blue of made belief. *Move*
rapidly toward the rising heat.

After an odd juke, the leaf, drained,
pauses on a stone whose alter-center
is the rare blue-shading white
of pale turquoise.
A lizard turns one eye
and studies the stone and leaf
for hours no one sees.

While resting,
cool. In cooling,
form wind. Without wind,
settle.

In time
the lizard rises
and leaves its marks of walking away,
records attitudes of legs and tails,
a sign with all the meaning
I need.

CHRISTINE GARREN

The Biopsy

When I closed my eyes
I thought about playing tennis with him
a long time ago on the deserted court, a mile from the ocean.
And the rallies that lasted a long time.
While the overhead clouds drifted like gulls. Thought not so
    much about him
as the field of us. The sun-embalmed afternoons
and sleepwalking for two years under the heavy pin oaks on the
    way to the pier
and fish houses. And then—and then—
the death of it.

The Heart

The child is being pushed by the mother, in the swing
that lifts over the deep lawn in May. Is being pushed towards
the tall hedge of bamboo
where the father must go
in a world that is houses and neighbors
gardens and furniture. Until the child floats backwards through
    the air
to be pressed again
towards the flowering bamboo hedge that moves in the wind like
    an animal.
Then the mother falls into the lilies, falls all the way backwards
into God.

Winds

We need centuries of them.
You wake up late in the morning,
the dark wind flowing through you,
and all day long it is the only thing that makes sense:
wind, that slides a hand under your boots
on the pavement and carries;
wind, that slices at the lips and cuts.
In it we listen
past voice—words irrevocably
flying to the front; future, flying back.
The problem of wind—
partially at our disposal—more than
partially not.

What I Looked at Today

1.

Today I walk, find
countless calla lilies.
How anything grows its own perfect white
and stays that way—unafraid
of world.

It is lovely, so I look.
It doesn't matter
what it thinks of me.

2.

This is what I've been given to look at.
I never chose to be here—
California gardens, riches.
There are brutal things. Like the sun.
How I have resisted this nature. Roses
most of all. (Lessons I did not want.)
But today I cut buds—common with thorns—
and place them on our dresser.
Inside, my husband says—*Isn't it amazing
how far they open up?*

I watch for days.
Is this what Job did?
Coming out of his world—didn't he
have to stare anew (for a little while)
wondering if beauty could hurt him?

CINDY GOFF

Meeting Mr. Right at the Rest Stop

He showed me brochures
for the last moment of my life.

He had done an elaborate makeup job on his wrists,
so it would look as if he had tried to commit suicide.

He gave me a ring, bright as the eyes
of a child on a stupid church trip.

Our families threw advice at the wedding.

When I had an orgasm, my hand opened wide
like I was picking up a toy.

When he was finished with me, I felt like an autopsy.

He kept whispering, "Yeti, Yeti," in my ear.

When I had nothing to say to him,
I always fell back on the shapes of countries.

I was sick of dusting
the skeletons of his claustrophobia.

I wondered if he would ever promote me to maid.

I was tired of hearts with wings.
I wanted a heart with a stone

tied around its leg,
so it would never

have to do jumping jacks

for anyone again.

In Chekhov

In Chekhov, everyone's unhappy—
this one loves that one who loves
someone else. The doctor, a fixture
of the plays, is always old as Chekhov,
who died young, must have felt himself
to be. And the aging writer, who also
resembles Chekhov, chases a girl

he will abandon soon and is stuck
with the habit of drawing out small
notebooks every so often, wanting
the youth he traded for fame. *Moscow,*
say the sisters, *is where we could be
happy,* knowing they will never
get there, too beautiful for happiness,

with feelings too keen, dreams,
like their upswept hair, too outdated—
their long dresses part of history.
Work, says one hero, *love,* says another.
No one can tell you if happiness
is anything but the opposite of
irony or being unprotected.

JAMES HAUG

25 at Dawn

Clock a few miles east on Jericho Turnpike—
how new asphalt levels the ride.

Consider too the foot-thick concrete slabs
(poured in the '30's or earlier)
we used to drive on, the road beneath the road.

Before that, plank:
two parallel rows of hemlock, four inches square—*sleepers,*
laid in three to four feet apart,

upon which eight-foot planks were placed unfastened.
A mixture of coarse sand, fine gravel, and dung

formed on the road a hard surface
which sped the delivery of produce and goods and pushed
the reach of commerce further east.

Beneath the planks, an Algonquin trail,
footpath from the East River to Montauk Point—

Fugitive landscape.
                    The sun is rising
over a flea market spread across the rolling flats
of a defunct drive-in,
mute speaker-poles poking up like stubble,

wind shaking down the corrugated steel panels of the deserted arena.

Hard to name it, a place that's no place, so populated,
    and unpeopled.
Nowhere to walk, and nowhere to walk to.

After the developer slapped together enough houses, he came up
with a solution: name the town after him.
We lived in the map fold, in the pocket of the Northeast.

So it was that a chickadee
with its hooked song
awakened me thirty-five years ago.

Today, as I look for an old girlfriend's house,
the road beneath the road carries me along.

I heard she's a parole officer now.
That house sold:
                it's all painted yellow.

78's

I've covered hundreds of miles in search of
the perfect song—records
often so ruined they sound buried
as if they were being played
under the floor. Along with 78's,
Stanley's Old
Furniture Store sold miniatures: homunculi,
chairs for mice, golf carts and threshers,
a pair of Guernseys
housed in a matchbox. I studied these
as a distillation
of size, an enormity I could pocket
and take with me. The relationships
their placement described said very little,
though as dust settled year
after year a story had emerged. Bankruptcies
and long evasive phone calls with bill collectors,
brothers who stood up
after a cup of coffee and never spoke
again. In the hills I've heard
lived the purest singers, miners
who came forth crying "You Are My Sunshine,"
fiddles that groaned like the last day
of fall, like an elevator descending
a dubious shaft. Out of gas
in a mountain town, Dock Boggs sang up enough
for supper, breakfast, and his tank.
Getting down the mountain was the easiest part.

JOHN HAZARD

Summer Witness, 1995

The first birds chirp again, as if they heard
the whole late July planet tilting with new law.
Goose honk and crow caw and squirrel jabber
are dawn light crawling up the huge maple trunk,
tinting rough gray wood till it glows,
green and mossy and tropical
in the tilted passing of planetary items.

This summer I have seen
a deer stroll across the yard, a buck,
one baby rabbit abandoned, stranded against a tree,
a large turtle on a dirt path, the back rim of its shell dug in,
in the woods a dead robin, eyes open, wings folded, formal,
the new neighbor's gray cat stalking every dawn,
two of his mice left in the yard,
my wife's new hair, downy, a baby's hair,
no wig, no scarf in the tilt of this day that moves
as if to evade my pen and its clumsy, bigger letters,
pressing harder, intruding—this may be the only copy.

And the old humans I have seen this summer,
all in one building, some sitting stunned, their stupefied questions
stared at everyone, everything, in the tilting planet,
while others hurry and hoard, thoughtless as squirrels—
then those two or three who calmly listen, like accepting monks
or a Great Blue Heron, camouflaged into one more
branch of leafless, dead, frog-home wood
among lily pads and carp and muck, the still or swaying reeds,
until he sees me watching,
and lifts, on huge and casual wings, away.

Downtown in Front of the Drugstore

Flat, jaw-dropped face of a Downs kid,
half-shut eyes, pale lids
like two oysters. A wide, squat body,
a slowness, he sits on a low wall, rocks
forward and back with his whole torso,
face blank with the rhythm of pushing
a stroller forward and back, that
soothing, shushing motion.

My baby waits at home; I quicken,
then passing, see in the stroller only a doll,
but enormous, a moon-faced rag doll
with lipstick mouth, black freckles,
yarn hair flagrant as poppies.
I walk on, he sways—nerves
flail their signals—we move, rocking
on accident's moonless tide.

Gray

She stood in the street, perplexed, as if she had just been dropped there. This was the late 1900's in a Western European city much like any other, when the streets at lunch hour teemed with office slaves, like herself, with their sandwiches slightly wet from sitting in ice all morning, and most of each month a cloud would cover the city, immovable and oppressive, wet all the way down to the pavement, wet in the fumes of buses and trucks slamming inches from the face.

She had gotten a temporary job working for an academic institution because of her nearly paranormal skills on a computer. Her hatred for the computer was part of her professional objectivity in dealing with their programs and systems. Sometimes the desire to kill a thing produces the profoundest understanding of it; it creates a powerful spell. Even now she was suffering from the inability to leave her computer work behind; to stop hating it and forget the case her boss had just dropped on her. She could not enjoy her lunch break.

What had happened was this. They were standing in the two-tiered office off a busy street that morning. The boss, a professor, and the office worker were both American, but he had a long-haired and sloppy look, along with a soft voice that somewhat masked his nationality. She wore the international student apparel that travels like mercury and her hair to her earlobes.

"While you are updating the system, I want you to keep your eye out for an error in there," the professor said. "It might be in the database. It might be human fallibility. The problem has existed for three years, so you have masses of material to plow through—three hundred files for each of those three years. And two different programs. But don't be daunted. The error is there somewhere."

"Why," she asked him, "is this so important? One error in three years is inevitable." She had never been asked to locate an error before; now it upset her.

"True, but our system is archaic. And the problem relates to a grade a woman received during the first year she was here and which is affecting her entire career. She will sue the institute—or bring us to court at least—if we can't prove that our grade was based on solid evidence."

"What kind of solid evidence?" she asked.

He explained—in the patient but remote tones of an academic— that the student, who had come over from America for one year, had received an A in a certain class. This excellent grade had given her the impetus to pursue a series of courses on her return to America that would lead to a career in some special kind of mathematics. However, somewhere along the line her A turned into a C, and this dropped her grade point average to a number that would put her out of the running for a top graduate school in her field.

"The written report she received with her A was apparently good, too," the professor said. "But at some point someone who worked in this office decided an error had been made, and her grade was dropped two points, turning up on her final evaluation as a C. By this time she had already left the country and spent another year and a half of her life operating on the assumption that she could pursue one career that now, of course, is closed to her. She can't go on to graduate school. The solid evidence would be hard copy—physical proof of this change in her grade."

"She must be really upset!" she cried, and her hand slapped at her cheek.

"Well, yes, to put it mildly. But we are unclear whether the new grade was based on new evidence that we received and stored somewhere—or whether the last girl working here screwed it up. And we have no way of tracing it humanly, by fax or phone, because the original grader and instructor has died and your predecessor has no recollection of this student. Usually girls like you are incredibly good at remembering these details."

The professor laughed and loosened his necktie awkwardly as if to acknowledge the completion of his first lecture in a long time.

"Let me tell you something," the office worker said. "With three hundred students a year—and the girl before me made a mess of the files—this is going to take me a long time. Couldn't we just— you know—tell the woman we made a mistake and give her the original A? I mean, this can't be worth the time."

The office worker looked up expectantly at his gray neck from where she was sitting at her desk.

"I mean, who's to know? I mean, I'll be working on the program anyway—and—if she is doing fine in her classes otherwise—why worry?" she asked.

"Well, this has occurred, of course, to me, but the case has gone so far, you see, she is obsessed with seeing the evidence, handing it to a lawyer and to the graduate institute that is now rejecting her. You understand. We can't fabricate the instructor's comments, and we also hope to learn from this error how not to repeat it. So you need to keep careful records of your research."

"If the instructor no longer exists, I'd give her a break," muttered the woman. "But then I'm not an academic."

She was soon left alone in the small, dark, thickly carpeted office. There were file cabinets stuffed with manila envelopes on her right. On her left a small window looked onto a little court and other office windows, lighted in the gray of noon. She had a large computer with a program in dazzling colors in front of her, and the name of the angry foreign student was scrawled on an envelope to the left of the computer, where her tea also sat.

She tugged at her hair as if, in response, a bell might ring in her brain. A musky smell hung around her, an air that was filtered through spotty light, violent light, a light that was sick-making but subtle—computer light. Snaky cords coiled from printer and computer down to the floor. She pressed her bare foot down on one and wondered if the Macintosh bitten apple sign referred to Eve. Forbidden bytes of knowledge. It struck her as ironic that she was seeking an original error inside the symbol of the first fruit bitten. These idle and ironic thoughts sidled through her consciousness while she worked, amounting to nothing. She was mesmerized by the light of the computer perhaps, or by the responsibility of her job, but nothing stronger than irony or mild empathy passed through her on a working day.

Outside that evening it was different. Her face was reflected everywhere later, walking around buildings. Her hair was like something illuminated underwater. The adolescent girls out on the street, as in Thomas Hardy's novels, and workers like herself, were always targets for male cunning and desire. No matter how intelligent and capable they were, there was a vulnerability to

their bodies—supple, athletic, less pretty in face than in figure—
that made the men rapacious, scheming, driven by a kind of
homoerotic (because twisted by shame for someone not fully
developed) desire. Androgynous in their long-waisted and sporty
gestures, these female workers were destroyed not just by men but
by time as a conspirator with the men—vacillation and the aging
process—while they lived in dread and increasing sorrow at miss-
ing something. Always looking, always arriving and seeking. She
knew that girls like herself felt that they might have taken the
wrong step on the first day of their independence and could never
retract that error.

Everyone in that decade was talking about God not existing in
the usual sense anymore. God did not engage with creation or
take sides or even care what happened on the last page of the
story. Existence was now experienced as a calamitous state, an
accident in space producing all the monkeys and bananas we have
grown to love, and it was up to people alone to mend mistakes
and abnormalities, to rebuild the machine from the inside.

The office worker began to wait with increasing irritation each
day for her lunch break when she could escape the tedium of her
quest—through manila envelopes stuffed with grade sheets, a
pandemonium of instructors' comments, ever-changing lists of
grade interpretations (what an A meant here was not what an A
meant there), and her assignment to enter and organize all this
information inside the Apple. She updated as she went along. The
mysterious complaining student, Rosa Liu, had not yet emerged
in all the papers, and weeks had passed. How could such a seem-
ingly efficient institution allow such chaos to develop under a
series of clever academics?
Lunch break meant fresh air, window-shopping, striding, star-
ing, eating, and emptying herself of an unwanted and inexplica-
ble desire for either love or praise. It was hard to tell the
difference. She believed that office slaves are so named because
they are a continuation of the economic model established in
plantation America. They work for a set of individuals who are
unknown to them and are managed by company men, like fore-
men, who are despised by both the owners and the slaves. In this

case the foreman was a professor who had been given this "plum" (a couple of years abroad) for a number of good reasons to do with his academic record, his scholarship, and his interest in students. She guessed that professors, despised by the administrators of the institution, have the same kind of vanity that foremen did on the plantations, believing themselves to be indistinguishable from the power source for whom they work and respected enforcers of the highest social values. They abuse the institution verbally and complain constantly, but this is only a symptom of their comfort in it. People who gripe aloud are rarely those who change social structures.

Phenomenal architectures swelled like stone fruits around her: a city built to last for eons, rounded carvings, fountains, thick walls, and marble floors. Yet the domestic interiors were like extensions of gardens, seedy and earthy with long, long windows flung open on the coldest days. The people who had constructed such glorious buildings and efficient aircraft for their last war could not make a warm house, a bottle cap that would work, or a box of juice that would open quickly and neatly.

They were a strange people, even to a person as well-traveled and sophisticated as she was. Their culture was them. For them. Around them. They wanted no other but this that they had formally constructed. They married each other, even if it was a cousin, in order to ensure that the culture remained uncontaminated, fresh. They loved themselves, though they had weak bodies and chins, and made fun of themselves, wrote satirically about themselves, and succumbed to poisonous bouts of depression expressed in the gloomy weather of their land. They created the weather that they were famous for: that damp slop that hung over everything came out of their cells. It emanated, was generated.

She fluffed up her hair, checking as if some father Midas had turned it to gold, had stiffened her in space. To be unheld and unconsoled was awful. Her flat was tiny and green, on the ground floor of an exceptional building occupied by very rich foreigners who worked in finance and politics. She watched television there, read, called a few friends, woke up depressed, and prayed. Both of her parents had died, she had no one but an aunt and a cousin who didn't know her at all. She was a world-soul, well-traveled, passed from school to school and land to land, her father an unreconstructed communist, her mother a pianist, both of them suicides. By the time she was sixteen, she had no place prepared for her on earth.

A couple of boys had come across her, and she had loved being held, fondled, and whispered to. She had believed that she would be rescued, adored, made safe—but in neither case did this occur. Now there was this professor who had a fleshy tender face, unlike the American faces she could spot from afar—those faces exploding with ego. He seemed recessive and bored, disillusioned by this "plum" he had been offered, pumping across the carpeting, shoes dragging. Often he stood behind her chair, facing her work on the computer, making comments, his hands resting near her hair, and she would feel herself seep downwards and ask him in a shaky voice about his family.

Finally one day she came on the missing file, and they were exuberant together and went to a restaurant to celebrate and study it. It was three pages of wrinkled and crushed paper, grade sheets, comments. At the time the student Rosa Liu was already a serious mathematics major. Here in these pages was the original A and the original comment from an instructor with an illegible signature (he was apparently deceased anyway), saying, "Fine work—absolutely one of my best visiting students."

Over plates of Caesar salad the professor and his assistant became increasingly perplexed and agitated by the comment. The other pages were from other instructors in her field, all praising her, giving her top grades, and saying what a pleasure she was in class. How did this one grade get changed into a C?

"I think it was a human error, made before I got here," said the woman, "and we should just change it here and now and let her deal with it that way."

"You seem to be impatient—a bit," said the professor, wiping oil from his chin.

"Oh, no. I like mystery, the regular part of the job is routine."

"You like it here? I can, I'm sure, arrange to have you kept on."

"Don't worry, I'm fine," she said unaccountably.

"Where's home?" he asked.

"I have none, that's the problem...," she said, hoping he would call her indispensable and make her feel wanted.

He studied her face briefly, then paid their check, and she followed him out onto the wet gray street. She particularly like the bones in his fingers, since they reminded her of her father, whose hands had been muscular from the labor they had endured. Yet her father had often said to her, "Everything is about power," as if his own life had been energetic and well-rewarded.

"I think you should keep looking for the error," the professor said to her over his shoulder, "but don't forget to update the system at the same time."

"That's what I was hired for . . . What should I be looking out for?"

"Probably it's a sheet of comments, like these ones, but sent later, maybe in an envelope still, and stuffed into the wrong file. You'll just have to rip everything apart. Do you mind? The last girl didn't have the patience."

They were at the bottom of the steps to the office.

"The salary is good," she replied. "Besides, I'm improving my own skills as I go along. By the time I'm done, believe me, there will be updated files and a new way of accessing them and a better way of entering the data."

"I hope so," he said grimly. "It will certainly be good on my record, if you get this sorted out. I'm always afraid this job was given to me as a form of gray-listing."

"Gray-listing? I've only heard of blacklisting."

"Age," he only remarked cryptically.

She answered the telephone, too, and sometimes talked to students who were worried or homesick. Usually, though, he did the counseling, and she would listen, suspended on her chair, to his voice in the next room; his kindness was palpable, he didn't judge. Other professors sometimes dropped in, and they would all go out for lunch or drinks, and she would hear their ironies, their bitter cracks about their work or their colleagues, and she would be astonished at his amendments to their snideness, the way he spoke no ill of others and expressed compassion for people described as idiots and jerks. Yet he never praised her.

She envied his wife and children. But she didn't covet him, she only desired to know that she was respected by him. Sometimes she thought it was physical love she desired, and she prayed that God would take away this hunger, and went to clubs with other office girls and pretended to be interested in anyone interested in her, but she wasn't. When he asked her, perfunctorily, to his house for dinner, she went obediently, but grieved throughout the occasion, watching the wife—as tall, flat, and serious as a door—and her clone daughter as they circled him with critical ease.

One day after Christmas—such a violent vacation—laden with obligation and images of the Saint of Capitalism, fat and red-furred and white and full...she went to the office, it was closed, and almost miraculously put her hand into the file that contained the missing document. Of course it was in the wrong file, one belonging to another student from another year. It was in an envelope, stamped and mailed from the northern city where Rosa Liu's university was, and it contained a note from the late professor, correcting his original grade.

I would like to correct a grade I gave to one of your students, Rosa Liu, who took my class in Theorems in the Spring of 1993. It turned out that she plagiarized her written information. Then she wrote what amounted to psychotic accusations about me, which I am sure she has sent you. It is clearly too late to do anything but change her grade—she has already left the country—and I only hope that she didn't employ the same methods in order to receive the high grades she did in other classes here. Her grade should be reduced to a C, which in our country is no pass, but in yours is a low pass, I believe. She did after all attend all the classes.

Now the office worker, alone—it was Sunday, and she had left after church to come to the office as if it needed her—sat staring into the empty streets. She could destroy this letter, never find evidence of a change in the woman's grade, and continue to work in the office until she really was indispensable. This way she could continue to be close to something she wanted, whatever it was.

As a child she had been very sensitive to her parents' mood swings, their addictions to alcohol and pills, and had eyed them like a little rabbit in a big field because they often behaved like aliens. Their eyes reddened and grew wet and heavy, and they slogged across carpets and dropped suddenly asleep. But she had unformed memories—traces in her behavior—of good happy times with them, being rocked, held, kissed, read to, shown to, and the reason she prayed was because of those times, because she prayed really to them in the other world, and it might as well have been God who also liked to hide behind things.

Now she pocketed the letter and left the office and went for a long walk. A few fancy stores were open, she saw herself as light reflected in glass at several points, and wondered if there were any knowledge possible outside of experience. She took a bus and got out near the professor's flat, walking past it, back and forth, a few times. His car was gone. Her own activity disgusted and discouraged her, and that night she went to a club and necked with a Lebanese man who was, like her father, a communist and spoke of Trotsky with mixed emotions. He said he was surprised that "a dumb blond would know about continuing revolution," and his finger snapped her panties.

Alone at home she considered suicide and following her parents to the place where they had gone. This was a common consideration.

She reread the note several times and wished she could talk to Rosa Liu about it, before deciding her next move. After all, what did she know about this plagiary, and if it really made any difference to the woman's abilities as a mathematician? Why did Rosa want so badly to find the evidence, if in fact it was incriminating, ruinous to her? She must have known what her crime was, and why her grade was changed. Why did the instructor, in his first letter, say that she was one of the best visiting students he had encountered if it weren't true? And what were Rosa Liu's so-called accusations?

The office worker wanted very much to destroy this letter. But some respect for facts made her hesitate. This respect was a kind of superstition. It was almost as if she imagined facts as bodies that could walk out of the chaos of time—even walk with a purpose—and that they could witness a false fact coming and steer surrounding events in a way that would release a kind of plague of lies. Indeed, out of revenge for her wickedness, the original fact would bend all first destinies into jammed-up paths.

Then she wondered if all this storing and collecting, which was embodied and embedded in the great leaden form of the computer, was perhaps driving her crazy. She felt a little uncoordinated mentally.

At work the next day she imagined herself showing the professor the letter and being pleased that he praised her for her diligence, for working on Sunday, and perhaps he would be worried that she might feel, now, compelled to quit the job, having discovered the root of the error. Don't quit, he might say, because now that you have updated the system, you are really indispensable, the only one who knows this thing in depth. You are all but an assistant registrar by now!

Pleased, she nonetheless didn't speak to him but went back into her office and turned on the computer, watching the colors pop up and wondering if colors like this would be reflected in a river. She gazed angrily into the screen, then returned to the files, hunched over them, determined to come to a decision about Rosa Liu. Her posture grew tense and threw sharp pains down her spine, and she began pulling out manila envelopes at random and spreading them around her on the floor, so that she could have greater ease sorting through them.

When the professor cast his shadow over her, from his position at the door, she looked at him with the same expression she had given the computer earlier. He removed himself, backwards, and she returned to her task. Days later, when she was still engaged in her pursuit through actual paper, on the floor, he insinuatingly wondered if she was still updating the computer system in the process of searching for this error. She told him that there was a basic flaw in the way the institute was processing grades, based on illegible notes from professors whose values and judgments bore no relationship to the home system.

"The only way," she said, "to make this work would be to acknowledge the radical difference between the systems and grade everyone who attended and did the work according to one universal standard—Task Completed Satisfactorily."

The professor laughed heartily, but the redness in his cheeks outlived the upturned shape to his lips. They argued for the first time. His voice grew loud, and he interrupted her, and said "Yeah yeah yeah" in impatient tones while she was explaining her point of view to him; he was in a hurry for her to stop talking, so he could talk better. She was on the floor, crouched, but her mind was outside, leaping up the steps of a store with spears of light shattering the time she was in.

Some people achieve a mystical perspective on the world by mental struggle, by unrelenting questioning of natural law, of time and imagination. Those lights that gathered around her protectively while she lived and walked were also part of her mind, extra parts. Now she crawled across the office floor past the professor's legs and told him she actually knew better than he about the failures in the grading system, because she was working with it daily. But he insisted on his perspective and on the need for maintaining equivalencies between universities in relation to a global vision. "We would be reverting to a kind of reverse snobbery if we let students get away without being graded according to the terms of the country they were in. The implications would be that we were just sending them over here to have fun."

"If the standards are different, how can the judgments be the same?" she muttered, then shut up. She grew depressed. But she kept up her hunt, daily, for some new piece of evidence. And then one night she found it, when she was alone, with the manila folders spilled on the floor under the colors of the computer and an overhead electric bulb. It was folded into long sections as if a child had been making a paper airplane from it. But the black e-mail print was immediately recognizable, in this case written like a poem in a narrow column.

Dear profeser in the rest room
you make me feel your big member
you pull my hair call it part of
the uncertanty world I was just there
to clean toilets to pay my education
but you stole my theorem
but said I was unworthy of you.
You stole my theorem for your use.
You stole it for your carer. Big Phd man
who done nothing for yers. No promotion!
You think I don't know you fail?
You don't care I died in industral acident
before I never maried my husband
he was no profeser but only loved him briefly.
Because of the one who came
you call these the laws of imigration a finger bone
to the one on the word procesor
a stick for the fil clerk fethers for the cleanng women
sex for this toilet washer who wrote a great theorem
you stole and you know the persen
who understans the problm is at the botom

of the barell I used to think
maths could solve anything profeser
but maybe you could help me find a new solution
or proof if you profer?
See no mater what I was respected in my country.

Rosa Liu

Now what could the office worker do with this information? She read and reread the e-mail several times. Her complexion silvered. She shut the door. It was drizzling on the dirty glass that looked out into an alley and across into other windows neon-lighted and filled with office workers like herself, facing full into the computer's screens.

What would influence her next move? Her parents' suicides? her belief in God? her Red upbringing? her loneliness? her need for the professor's love? her hatred of the computer? her hatred of the professor? the rain? the lights? the light? her temperament? her brain? I'll just think awhile, she decided. And she thought about calling the department at the university where Rosa Liu had been accused of plagiary. She wondered what story they would give her. But when she proposed doing this, the professor told her he had already called the department, and they had been close-mouthed, impenetrable. But she didn't quite believe him, because of the way his eyes were lowered and looking to the right.

For the next week she cleaned up the files from the floor and noted with some pleasure the effects of her work, her innate sense of sequence, so that the envelopes looked and now were in a form that no other office girl could fail to understand. And the computer system could now pop up the name of each former student including a grade point average and the classes they took and who taught them, in a matter of seconds. Yet with each grade she entered for this year's class, she made a little change, raising the grade a point or two. Why not? Sometimes it is almost intolerable that order, being so impersonal, is simultaneously so brutal.

That same evening she recalled the way God parted the waters, saying: "Let there be a dome in the midst of the waters, and let it separate the waters from the waters." And she felt a fellowship with this action. She hunched into her computer posture, face fixated on the glass as if she were seeing the arrival of warplanes over a swaying horizon, while in her lap she nervously attached Rosa Liu's e-mail to the professor's letter with a clip. She would reveal the results of her tireless search in the early winter darkness as they were each leaving to go home. The professor would be embarrassed because he would have guessed it was something like this. And so would she. And the embarrassment would bind them weirdly as they went up the stairs and together changed the grade to an A. The fact was, at her age, she would have a hard time finding a permanent new job.

Elegy for a Rain Salesman

for John Engman (1949–1996)

Dear friend, I heard tonight by phone
of that ghost bubble in your brain.
It was not the pearl of balance one fits
between lines in a carpenter's level
to make something plumb, but a blip
in a membrane that burst so now
       your fine brain is dead—

that city of mist that nests in your skull
will never again flicker with light.
By air-phone, I talked to your mom tonight
flying the red-eye home. Through static
her voice stayed calm, wondering when
to unhook the hospital's bellows.
       She thought—I swear—a trip

to the beauty shop would help, and John,
how you'd have cackled at that.
That winter after Europe when I was broke
and camped on your sofa for months,
that dusky laugh kept me alive.
Each night in a menthol fog we drank
       till last call.

Once staggering home, we stopped
to crane up between buildings, lines of windows
rising away in rows. We listed in wonder,
leaning together like cartoon drunks.
You pointed out a rectangle of sparkled sky—
beauty's tattered flag—we pledged allegiance to—
       mittens over our heaving chests,

cold to break your teeth on,
a jillion stars foretelling none of this. Your mom said
your last sight on earth was your own face
in the shaving glass—that hermit's flat on Colfax Ave.
where I watched you tape to the bathroom wall
the first *New Yorker* rejection of hundreds.
    So that monocled asshole

on the letterhead must have recurred
like wallpaper four hundred times
behind your moon face rising. Freeze
that frame. Let me hold awhile
with imagined hands that face,
as you might have briefly held that day
      the worn oval of soap—

idly, with no thought of its vanishing.
Let me watch you shape in your palm
a frail Everest of shaving foam,
then smear yourself a snowman's face
with coal eyes staring out. The infinite night
that drew our drunk salute has now
      bled into that skull,

glazed its porcelain with spider cracks
like a Grecian urn. Our time's
run out. No epitaph on which to safely land
appears in my oval porthole. The prairie slides beneath me
white as any page. And rain has hardened
into ticking sleet. Sleep, friend, as I cannot, reading
      the lines you left,

streaking behind you like a comet's tail:

...I wanted to be a rain salesman,
carrying my satchel full of rain from door to door,
selling thunder, selling the way air feels after a downpour,
but there are no openings in the rain department,
and so they left me dying behind this desk—adding bleeps,
subtracting chunks—and I would give a bowl of wild blossoms,
some rain, and two shakes of my fist at the sky to be living...

On Roses and the Cheapness of Talk

After I'd filled the crystal vase with water, I thought
of your ancient mother, who came once
like a witch from a fairy tale
to curse our uncertain union,
how she stood at my sink and lectured
on cutting stems at a slant under water
　　　　so the blooms would last—

this after weeks of oceanic quiet you bobbed in
(muddy gloom). And though you resembled
a grown man at full power, and though
she finally flew back to her cold island,
I watched you wither under her scorn
and could not infuse you, for your own spine
　　　　skewered you on its spit.

So you took to our bed, doped up and dull,
and through smeary glasses read book
after book to block out the loud world.
And despite ministrations (the meals I brought
on a tray) you could not stand whole or sustain
any small kindness. That's why at the end
　　　　you were shipped home

to that bitch who whelped you and still keeps you tethered
to the stake of her fury, and that's why
after I'd sprinkled the vase water with aspirin
I'd ground with a spoon, I thought and thought and
thought better of it, so those blossoms you sent
got beheaded and Jiffy-packed back, for love's
　　　　not a gilt-edged storybook:

Talk is cheap.

Avoid Eye Area

Sometimes I have to squint to see clear
and used to think this a fault of light—
God's failure to beam the intended world
bright enough on the brain pan. Now I know
it's age, my own worn optical works
that blur leaves to smudge. Justice
      wears a blindfold,

and the firing squad captive whose chest
under its rope cross explodes in red flower.
And Eros also. When you were a sea away
I could close my eyes and picture your profile
to fit on a Roman coin, face bent
to a lamplit page, skull full
      of rare creatures.

But up close your jaw became horselike, mouth
pouting and girlish. Your silences
not abrim with wisdom, but cold,
meant to stave off the lived-in world.
Though you liked to fuck me well enough,
at the end I could only bear that from behind,
      so I was blind

to what you'd warped into. After I'd sent you off
I wept till my lids swelled closed.
Now I keep my eyes open, even in shower steam
when I rinse the last scum off and my flesh
wants to invent some lied-about ghost.
It's my hand carries fire through the soap foam,
      my own streaming head

makes the story. The shampoo bottle blares
the square-lettered truth I now heed rather
than your letters' curlicued lies: Caution:
      avoid eye area.

MAURICE KILWEIN GUEVARA

Memorial Day

My father, an American, was singing in dialect over the grave of my great-grandmother. The sun was setting. The country was in another war. My mother was planting nasturtiums over Nonna's grave. Her green skirt was shorter than the grass. A northern shrike was piercing a songbird on a thorn of barbed wire. The old veterans had already pushed the Catholic cemetery gates closed when the brown bats started to ricochet in the violet-tangerine sky.

The twins' first memory is of silence and the slight trembling of semen.

STEVE KOWIT

The Black Shoe

Newlyweds, up at the Del Mar station, saw the woman
stumble & fall, & ran back to pull her to safety,
the train bearing down. For a thousand feet
north of the point of impact, investigators found
parts of a briefcase, sketches of gowns,
a low-heeled black shoe. From the White House,
the President screaming for blood.
A quarter million American boys already shipped
to the Gulf: no doubt some of the kids
from the base: Mike Santos & Tracy & Kevin, horsing
around like they used to in class—a football
spiraling over the Saudi Arabian sands. At night,
unable to sleep, tossing in bed, I hatch extravagant plots.
I am determined that not a single one of my students
shall die; not a single Iraqi infant be orphaned
or murdered. Such are the feverish thoughts that spin
through my head in that fugue state
before sleep lifts me out of myself & carries me off.
In the morning, however, it isn't the President
circled by microphones screeching for war
that throbs in my head, but that unstoppable train
& the fact that both women were killed: the one
who'd just gotten married, reaching her arms
to the arms of the one who had stumbled
& fallen. It won't let me rest. That briefcase.
Those bloody sketches of gowns. The black shoe.

I Rendezvous with Jim & Lenny at The Barnes

We swept up everything in sight: gobbled up Soutines, Bonnards
Modiglianis. Lenny snagged Monet's boat studio.
Jim seized that mauve felicity of creamy lovers: *Le Bonheur
de Vivre.* I took that terrifying Van Gogh
nude, horrific & farouche, all poverty & pubic hair & suffering.
Together after all those years—three hebephrenic
& disheveled antiquarian collectors
from the Dumbbell Nebula.
The museum-goers gave us a wide berth.
The guards eyed us suspiciously & shifted feet.
At closing time we slipped into our coats & left
our acquisitions where they'd hung,
& traipsed out into an icy dusk.
In Philadelphia, on Earth, all afternoon,
it had been snowing: a foamy, plush, untouched
meringue of snow, all lacy-blue beneath the streetlights,
blanketing the lawns & trees & roofs
& roads of Lower Merion—flakes huge as pie plates
floating all about us as we clowned
& schmoozed the way we used to
carry on back in Manhattan
down on 6th Street
in the old days: nothing now but tiny strokes of silver-
gray & orange & maroon, receding
past the middle distance—rapturous,
maniacal—high-stepping through a blizzard of exquisite light.

ADRIAN C. LOUIS

Adiós Again, My Blessed Angel of Thunderheads and Urine

Ah, so there you are, somewhere between the
Demerol and the morphine, silently emptying
my catheter jug. Don't do that, I want to say,
but my voice is lost from two weeks on the
ventilator. Baby Girl, I want to say hello, say I
know your name, say how much I've always
loved you, but only a rasp comes and then you
are gone forever again.

I know I've got a crinkled picture of you
boxed somewhere in my shuttered house.
The image is as foreign as it is faded.
Somewhere west of Tulsa, you are leaning
against a black Bug, smiling and pointing
at a remarkable formation of thunderheads
that tower and bluster miles past heaven.
Your long, black hair dances below your waist.
Your worn navy bell-bottoms are snug against
your perfect legs, your strong, loving hips.
And after I snap the photo, you tell me that
you're going back to nursing school.
Me, I'll wander in the wilderness for thirty years
before I see you again, and then, it will be only
for a brief minute while you empty my urine
bucket and I try to cough up words that
will not come like the flashing pain beneath
my sutures that signals healing and wonder.

Dear Homeboy

There's a stealthy, sort of leopard-
like knocking at my door
tonight I half
wish were you, but the sky's
grainy violet and no one's out there
loitering darkly like a dent.
Know what's going down?
Total eclipse of the moon,
Kid—it's pretty dim
out, just
the gas station's block
of light like the landmark
at the world's
end: *Jump off here.*
If you were there you'd use it
to check out your reflection
in the hood of someone's car.
You'd use the neighbor's zinnias
to wipe the street life
off your feet, use
your condition as an alibi,
It couldn't have been me, man,
I'm, like, dead!
You'd consider knocking, take on
that shrewd look you always
got to hide a mind just half
made up, one hand idly
questioning the spot
around your ribs where blood
streaked out onto the asphalt
and turned black, *looked*
black, in the liquor store blur
and bulb of ambulance. Look

up: a tablet dissolving in blue
mist, or mauve. I could swear
something sauntered to my door.
The moon's half gone—I
know the feeling, sure. And you,
you're gone more.

R. J. MCCAFFERY

Chaos Theory and the Knuckleballer

for Tim Wakefield

On the mound you stand—just so—
exhale—so—throw at the same spot
over and over. There's only one way
to toss a knuckleball, near-impossibly simple;
your fingernails flick it
at the distant lozenge of the catcher's mitt,
but it must be thrown so evenly
the ball won't spin at all,
sixty feet six inches from hand to plate,
it can't rotate, not once.
At the end, it turns a half inch
so when the slight braking surface
of its raised stitched seam
shears against the stream of air
the ball plows through,
that change in flow will kick it aside—not much—
enough for a bat to swipe over, under, just to the left
of where the ball was. Or not. Somedays,
it's like trying to throw an oak leaf across the street
into your neighbor's half-closed mailbox.
Somedays it's good: you're on; just
that the ball perversely dips and skews
straight to the bat—right out of the park.
Or the ball won't break, just hangs
like a bright piñata.
Somedays it's perfect.
You can't hold runners for a damn,
floating that ball towards home like a soap bubble,
but most will wait anyway,
for the ball to lunge away from the bat
into the dirt, carom off the catcher's shin-guard,
and roll—like an evil bunt—into the on-deck circle.

Anything too good by a hair, or not good enough,
kills you. After a shutout (or single-inning debacle)
reporters want to know *Why? What happened?*
As the press-corps questions swirl around you
and the baseball that nestles like a Buddha in your glove,
you sense a slight breeze, an eddy so weak
it can barely sift through heat rising off the dirt.
A drop of sweat left on the ball? A stray mosquito?
The fat guy in the fourth row who blew on his coffee?
Who knows? Who knows how this pitch makes itself?
They say, to Jehovah, men were tools: Samuel
a sword, Isaiah a trumpet. What are you
to a knuckleball that pulls the world into itself?

JEFFREY MCDANIEL

The Wounded Chandelier

I went into a bar and ordered a childhood dream.
A woman came in and sat down next to me.

She was rather lanky for an amputee.
A voice said *She's too shallow to dive into.*

You'll break your noose on her concrete psyche.
I didn't listen. As a way of shattering the ice,

I told the story about the hemophiliac
who went bungee jumping, how his body

was this delicate sack of blood, bouncing
up and down in the air. I found myself

whispering things like *I only have eyebrows
for you.* She asked me to take her home.

I carried her promises up the stairs.
They were as fragile as light bulbs.

I was gonna defy gravity in her celestial body
but I had performance anxiety, so I wrote *Baby*

Jupiter in black Magic Marker on her forehead
and plummeted back into the bar.

The First One

Who knows what led me there—a twelve-year-old
leading my eight-year-old brother and his overnight guest

into the one clean room of that four-story brownstone
and plunging into the booze while our parents slept.

Maybe it was genetic curiosity, colliding with vodka,
a fifth of cheap Russian, and scorching a tunnel to our guts

as we quivered on the Oriental rug, passing the bottle
beneath the fancy paintings that held the walls up.

Consequence was a planet whose orbit we couldn't respect.
When the clear stuff got finished, red wine came next

with little bits of the cork I wedged down with a knife
bobbing like chaperones forced to walk the plank.

The room started flipping like a pancake. We dropped
glass anchors from that third-story porthole

transforming the neighbors into a frenzy of phone calls.
Who knows what emotions my parents were wearing

but whatever they said didn't make any sense
as we wiped our lips and spiraled into black.

H. BRUCE MCEVER

On the Road

I love early mornings in a new hotel,
traveling west and up on East Coast time,
before room service starts delivery,
searching the lobby or even down in the kitchen for coffee,
to greet dawn with the night clerk,
starting his wake-up calls.
I find a paper from the bundle by the revolving door
and a town map from the tourist's rack,
to discover where I am and what's happening,
having missed the previous day, sequestered
with clients in a windowless conference room.

I hardly notice a busboy picking up
last night's glasses and emptying ashtrays,
to start the lobby over with a worn smile by seven.
I begin to feel oddly comfortable
before the stir of day,
unhurried and almost at home
in the contrived elegance
of overstuffed couches, old marble, and mirrors.

I wonder how much of my life
has been spent, just like my father's,
in rented rooms and strange beds,
with our precious time
neatly folded and packed
into suitcases and carried
between the unforgiving schedules
of people and planes?

The Wreck

Again on the highway with tears in my eyes, cadenced by rhythm of concrete and steel, music of cloud vapor, music of signs—Blue Flame Clown Rental/Color Wheel Fencing—again overcome, again fever-driven, transported among the pylons and skidmarks of the inevitable, sirens and call-boxes of a life I have laid claim to with a ticket found by chance in the pocket of a secondhand overcoat. And if it should come to that, if my fate is to be splayed on an altar of steel, heart held forth on an Aztec dagger of chrome, if this, then still I say it was beautiful, the freedom and speed with which you conveyed me, the way and the will, and I won't renounce the road's acrid rubber or deny the need that sent me there, and I will not regret the purpose, the vehicle, the white line, the choice, and I will not mistake the message for the voice.

The Mayor

The light that woke the mayor made him think
of town. It was a pale pink light ticked out

by a palpitating bulb
that droned above the empty road he lived on.

He sat upright in bed,
noticed his posture,

how his jutting head
sought equilibrium and not much else.

God was far off. And, like an enemy,
the town was all around.

The sound of the several mills
was nothing but a funeral sob. The hills

were creeping with cattle,
and the cattle with liver fluke.

His heart was beating this way: stop, stop, stop...
God was far off. The town was all around.

Confusing Weather

The sun came to in late December. Spring
seemed just the thing that flattered into bloom
the murdered shrubs along the splintered fence.
The awnings sagged with puddles. Roads were streams.
Wet leaves in sheets streaked everything with rust.
The man who raked his lawn transferred a toad
too small to be a toad back to the woodpile.
In the countryside, he thought he spied the trust
that perished from his day to day relations.

His head was like a shoe box of old pictures,
each showing in the background, by some fluke,
its own catastrophe: divorce, lost friends,
a son whose number he could not recall—
this weather, nothing but a second fall,
ending, if somewhat late, just how fall ends.
Each day that week he sat outside awhile
and watched his shadow lengthen, disappear.
Then winter followed through its machinations,
crept up and snapped the head off of the year.

Requiem Shark with Lilies

Sailor boy in pantaloons guides his jacaranda
caravel through a labyrinth
of skulls, lichens bleeding in fontanels,
Easter winds
spraying heliotropes with ammonia.
Another makes a halo
stirring sand in brine that has preserved
a martyr's spleen 1,000 years.

St. Agnes sweeps the beach with coco fronds
collecting crossfish,
aureole urchins, angels' quills.
Jumps over a small requiem shark
half buried in wet sand:
its transparent body barbed with diamonds,
ten lilies suspended inside a glass

womb. Breaking the membrane with a weathered
pelican's beak, she tingles
as formaldehyde spills
down to her calcareous toes. One flower
begins to dig a burrow,

flailing iridescent petals very fast.
St. Agnes snatches the lily,
putting it in her clenched hand, which secretes
burning nectar through
the pistil; two stamens—long, spiculed—
squeeze her ring finger until it's blue.

She shakes her hand furiously,
its grip becomes tighter, the horny-beaked
stigma punctures
her fingertip, implants black ovules
that mix with her own blood
as it shoots over breakers. Gust shatters the arc,

the lily dies; rainbow droplets coagulate
coating seeds that germinate
inside fish bellies, alive in purgatory's trenches,
then migrate home with their hosts
at the start of Lent and breed on Easter Sunday.

W. S. MERWIN

Purgatory XVII

—a translation of Dante Alighieri's Purgatorio, *Canto XVII*

Remember, reader, if ever high in
   the mountains the fog caught you, so you could see
   only as moles do, looking through their skin

how when the humid, dense vapors begin
   to grow thinner the sphere of the sun
   finds its way feebly in among them,

and your imagination will easily
   picture how, at first, I came to see
   the sun again, already going down.

So, keeping pace with my master's trusted
   footsteps, out of a fog like that I came
   when the beams on the shore below were already dead.

O imagination, that sometimes steal us
   so from things outside us that we do not
   notice if a thousand trumpets sound around us,

who moves you if the senses give you nothing?
   A light moves you, in the heavens forming
   by itself, or by some will that guides it downward.

Of her impious act who changed her own
   shape to that bird's who most delights in singing
   the form appeared in my imagination

and at this my mind became so gathered in
   upon itself that nothing from without
   came then that was taken in by it.

Then there rained down, in the high fantasy,
    one who was crucified; scornful and fierce he
    looked out, and so he was about to die.

Around him were the great Ahasuerus,
    Esther his wife and Mordecai the just,
    who in his words and what he did was faultless.

And as this image broke up on its own
    like a bubble when the water is gone
    from under it, out of which it was made,

there rose into my vision a young girl weeping
    bitterly, and she was saying, "O Queen
    why did your anger make you want to be nothing?

You have killed yourself not to lose Lavinia;
    now you have lost me. I am the one, Mother,
    who grieves that your ruin comes before another's."

As sleep is shattered when a sudden
    new light strikes on the closed eyes, and though
    broken, it flickers before it is all gone,

so my imagining fell away from me
    the moment that a light greater than any
    we are used to struck me in the face.

I was turning to see where I was
    when a voice said, "The way up is here,"
    recalling me from any other purpose,

and made my will full of such eagerness
    to see who it was who had spoken, as
    cannot rest until it is face to face.

But as at the sun which weighs our vision down
    and veils its own image with excess,
    so my own strength was not enough for this.

"This is a divine spirit guiding us
   on the way upward without our asking him,
   and with his own light keeping himself hidden.

He treats us as a man does his own kind,
   for he who sees the need and waits to be asked
   already says 'No' unkindly in his mind.

Now to such welcome let our feet comply;
   let us try to go up before nightfall,
   for then we cannot until the return of day."

So my leader said, and we turned our footsteps,
   I along with him, toward a stairway,
   and as soon as I was standing on the footstep

I felt close to me something like the moving
   of a wing fanning my face, and heard *"Blessèd are
   the peacemakers* who are without evil anger."

Already the last rays which night follows
   had risen so far above us that the stars
   were appearing on all sides around us.

"O my strength, why this melting away?"
   I said in myself, feeling the force of my
   legs as it came to be held in suspension.

We had come to where the stairs went no higher
   and there we stopped, fixed, in the same way
   a boat is when it arrives on the shore.

And for a little I listened to find whether
   I could hear anything on the new circle,
   then I turned and said to my master,

"My kind father, tell me what offense
   is purged on the circle where we are?
   Let your words not be still although our feet are."

And he said to me, "The love of good which falls
    short of what it owes is restored just here;
    here is plied again the sinfully lax oar.

But in order that you may understand it more
    clearly, turn your mind to me, so you may
    gather some good fruit from our delay."

"Neither Creator nor creature ever,"
    he began, "was without love, my son, whether
    natural or of the mind, and you know this.

The natural is always without error
    but the other can err by choosing the wrong
    object or having too much or too little vigor.

While it is turned toward the primal good,
    controlling the secondary as it should,
    it cannot be the cause of sinful pleasure,

but when it twists toward evil or pursues
    the good with more or less zeal than it owes
    what is made labors against its maker.

Thus you can understand that love must be
    the seed in you of every virtue and
    of every act that deserves punishment.

Now, because love can never turn its face
    from the well-being of its subject, there is
    nothing that is able to hate itself.

And since a being by itself, cut off from
    the First One, cannot be conceived,
    all creatures are prevented from hating Him.

It follows, if I distinguish correctly,
    that what is loved is evil for the neighbor;
    this love is born in three forms in your clay.

There is the one who hopes he will excel
   by pushing down his neighbor, and for this
   longs only to see him fallen from his greatness.

There is the one who fears losing power,
   favor, honor, and fame, if surpassed by another
   which so grieves him that he loves the opposite,

and there is the one who feels such shame from
   an insult that he turns greedy for vengeance;
   such a one is impelled to plot another's harm.

For these three forms of love, down there below
   they weep. I would have you think of the other now
   which pursues the good in a corrupted way.

Every one perceives a good confusedly
   in which the mind may rest, and longs for it
   and so each one struggles to come to it.

If the love is half-hearted, that draws you to see it
   or to acquire it, this is the terrace
   that punishes you, after proper repentance, for it.

There is another good that makes no one happy.
   It is not happiness; it is not the Good
   Essence, the fruit and root of every good.

The love that abandons itself to this excess
   is wept for in three circles above us,
   but as to how it is ordered in three ways

I say nothing, so you may find it for yourself."

Hats Off

War's hell begins
with a parade, high-stepping
girls, the flag's harem,
Old Glory on its leash.

In a corner of the flag
is a token bit of night.
We round up the stars,
same as the boys.

A blood-red flag—
blood-blue, blood-white.
Reality's standard
must never touch earth.

Lining the streets,
cheering, we forget
how full of famous
bullet holes we are.

KIRK NESSET

Time on the Down of Plenty

On Slaughter Beach I lay me down
on the sand between surf and calliope, there
where oceania meets glitz: plastic

mosques and minarets and transvestals, sub-
verts, countersexuals—Spanky Sparklenuts,
Afterbirth Boy and Crab Apple, Candace

the Grimace and She-Who-Eats-Only-Fish.
Nighttime it was, brine-sour, my head sunk
in shadow. Above, boardwalkers walked—catcalls

and titters. Such was my time on the down
of plenty; such is my way when inwardness
knells. How had I let myself poison

my passion? How had I failed to feel,
knees in the dust? What's done's done, said
my head—just do what you do. Mingle

with toothless epicures; enough moral
engorgement. The camel and gnat strain on
as they must. The sea, neon-tinged, hisses.

And the misshapen champion—feckless, un-
daunted, plucked—cavorts in his fiberglass grotto,
flexing his liver, his terrible guts.

STEVE ORLEN

Gossip of the Inner Life

My good friend who these days despises the newspapers
Complains this isn't news but gossip,
                              a talking down,
In brief sidebars, in the mathematics of
The intellect, from the highest
To the lowest common denominator,

The front pages with their treaties signed and breached
In an afternoon, the borders
Fixing and unfixing themselves

Like pieces in a jigsaw puzzle a child
Forces into place
On a boring, rainy April morning,

All of which reads, he says, like hieroglyphic scum
On top of this great pond,
                              while underneath,
He does not say, all that lives
Swims a slow and noble, ordinary, translucent life,

And all that dies
                    falls to the bottom and becomes food.

I don't want to sound like the insensitive big shot
With his small ideas, but it's not
The mass killings in the world's fields
With reductive mathematics
                              that matter as much
As that principled woman
In the second section who refused to do her housework
For ninety-seven days
                         to prove a point. What might

She have been thinking the moment her grudges
Turned to a firm resolve, the second her hand

Picked up the dust mop and began its familiar
Sway and dance
                    across the floor, then stopped?
Do people grin
When they're alone? If we are to go on swimming,
We need to know that.
                    It's not the ears
The Colonel collected from his tortured dead
And swept from the coffee table in a gesture
Of contempt to terrorize the visiting reporter,

But how an ear might have felt if only the reporter
Had thought to bend and gently pick one up
And lay her mouth down
                    to ask for the gossip of death.
Break the ice, human nature oozes out,
                              that poetry
Somebody called "the gossip of the inner life."

John Clare, the mad and minor
                         rural English lyric
Realist, would have loved it, would have lived it,
As he in fact did, in
Poems Descriptive of Rural Life & Scenery,

Gossip of the badger, the fox,
Of maids and maidens
                    and the *Mary* he made up
To remind us of the purity of unrequited love.

What I remember, besides a few quaint, specific
Poems he wrote
                    that never made the evening news,
Is that he once escaped the asylum and walked
Six days eating grass and bugs and weeds

From Epping home to Northampton, and believed
He was the great Lord Byron himself,
                                    "mad, bad,
And dangerous to know."
                        Imagine, my friend,
You are John Clare as Lord Byron opening
The mansion doors
                    at 9 a.m., and receiving every guest,
Honored and dishonored alike, John Clare as
The filthy peasant with his hair slicked back

Sitting at table with John Clare as Lord Byron
Who had just come back from hunting grouse and snipe.

And what are grouse and snipe? you should ask.
It's important.
                And what did they say, one madman
To another?
            "What's new?"
                        Which is another way of saying,
What's the interior gossip?
                        Who would one day say,
"...now I only know I am, that's all."
And the other would reply, "What! What!"

Pastoral

We don't want to be shown, in photographs sent home,
What the poet saw that summer, that evening
In the mountains with the shepherds, that unspoiled
Landscape with its caves and weathered ruins,
Nor to be retold, in long scribbled letters
After the wine was drunk, drunken revelations
Of the shepherds' joys and troubles, no matter
How deeply felt (that baby named after that mother
Who took off and moved in with that man from town),
In the homogenous tongue or in one
Of the vulgar dialects, spoken by the shepherds
Like simple folk devolved from gods and heroes.
And we don't want the clouds in all their usual
Depictions, looking like quaint childhood animals,
But would rather he simply counted them, in numbers,
Our prime inheritance, those first useful abstractions,
And want the shapes of the numbers as carved in runes
Whose code hasn't yet been broken from their stones.
We require of our poets what has been forgotten,
Nor the details of battles lost and won,
But their essences, composed in an addendum
Borrowed from Horace—*arrogance, reluctance, perfume*—
Composed while walking down the *Via Negativa,*
That infinite progression of what isn't. We want
What has been made up, or dreamt, or misunderstood,
What the poet later tried to tell a friend, but failed,
So lied: fog, smoke, echo, breath, for it does us
Little good to hear either the awful truth
Or the pleasant. Lacking that, a list of flowers will do.

On Poets, Poets Teaching, and Poetry: Notes from a Journal

Much has been written about the influence of the academy on the writer who teaches there. But what about the influence a writer may have on the academy? On our way to the airport after her visit at my campus, Lucille Clifton, speaking of poets who teach, asks: "Who else can teach students about the need to serve something larger than themselves?" Later, she remarks on the limits of the academy's approach to education: "It teaches one way of knowing," she says, "and it's the easiest way." Clifton adds she no longer felt ashamed of lacking an academic degree once she realized that, having none, she was better able to show students other ways of knowing.

*

Could it be that creative writing has become so popular in colleges today because of our students' need to reclaim the personal and moral uses of language in a period when advertising has so corrupted it? On some level, the students in my classes at the University of Maine at Farmington feel this need, I think. Consequently, I take satisfaction from the main lesson in language they learn there: telling the truth.

*

"I don't know how to fill up all those pages," says one of my best student poets, now taking a fiction class. Time will tell whether she's too much a poet to be shown the ways of fiction, as a few students seem to be. But it is clear that poets think differently than do fiction writers. They see what they see in a flash—a sudden insight that gathers a cluster of associations—and their thinking, unlike the episodic and linear thought of the story writer, is kaleidoscopic, concentric.

*

How, then, to write the narrative poem? Best to find an action that may be explored in a variety of ways as it unfolds, so that what happens in the poem has the sense of being simultaneous, as

in, say, Rich's "Diving into the Wreck," or Bishop's "The Moose."
Best to combine the narrative and the lyric.

*

Elizabeth Bishop, while still a student at Vassar and trying to find a way to describe the poetry she writes and wants to write, says in a letter there are two kinds of poems—those "at rest" and "in action"—and adds that she favors the latter kind. To explain what she means by "action," she refers in this instructive passage to her models, the writers of Baroque prose: "Their purpose was to portray, not a thought, but a mind thinking.... They knew that an idea separated from the act of experiencing it is not the idea that was experienced. The ardor of its conception in the mind is a necessary part of its truth."

*

How different Elizabeth Bishop is from the poet who must work for a living. I teach and then return home to grade papers. Bishop writes a letter to say she's thinking of buying a clavichord—then buys one, taking lessons on it because she feels this will help her poetry.

*

How does one respond to the maddening complaint of students that poetry which touches on sorrow is "depressing," when it is clear they speak for the American culture that made them?

I am told that a Russian does not, like the American, say "Fine" when asked how he is. He uses the time-honored gesture of the hand that says "So-so" or "It could be worse." The response suggests an awareness of life's difficulties, which we as human beings know well, wherever we may live. It does not insist on happy endings or the need to provide them; it suggests that things do not always come out well, that life includes not only affirmation but tragedy. It is not mythic; it is realistic.

Can anyone deny how dangerous our compulsion to affirm is to the affairs of the nation? Unable to address our complex social problems—the widening gap between rich and poor, the racial troubles, the murderous acceleration of American life—with a confident smile, we tend to deny them, insisting that "we're number one" in the great country of happy outcomes, whether that country exists or not.

The student who finds poetry that is grim or sorrowful

"depressing" must be shown the impoverishment of his American mythology—perhaps by introducing him to his own national tradition in literature, including novelists from Melville to Faulkner, playwrights from O'Neill to Williams, and poets from Dickinson to Rich—developing early and late a tragic vision that might mature the nation.

Or show the student—through his writing itself—how his truest work comes from dealing with the flawed world as he really knows it, beyond the clichés of American happiness.

*

I tell my fiction students if anyone says or does something I can use in a story, it's mine, with no apologies, says Sharon Sheehe Stark, and she's right to tell them so. We are all obligated to give our stories and our poems what they need to live. One must decide whether one wants to be polite or to be a writer.

*

Here is Galway Kinnell seated among students, yet several states and countries away from them, in his own time zone, as he observes the young man asking the question. In his own time, from his own time zone, he responds.

In the car on the way up from the airport, he is closer, though still, and I sense always, apart. We have a lively conversation about the tired syntax of contemporary American poetry—that generic sentence that begins with a declarative and follows up with qualifiers, often participial phrases or verb complements or objects in a series, direct or prepositional. We agree that Dickinson and Frost offer fine models of the delayed verb, and of a less predictable syntax in general.

As we near my house at the end of our trip, Kinnell speaks of his search for a way to refer to Frost at his upcoming investiture as Vermont's Poet Laureate, and I suggest he read Frost's short poem "On Being Chosen Poet of Vermont," which he does not know. Standing in my kitchen to read the poem for the first time out of my Frost Collected, he nods and smiles, in the time zone of his delight.

*

Galway Kinnell does as Frost used to do: delivers his poems from memory. Patricia Smith does the same, insisting that when poets address their audiences directly, saying their poems and not reading them, they make a stronger impact. Yet the page has its value as a prop. In moving his eyes from page to audience and back again, the poet is demonstrating that his reading is about more than the exchange between him and the audience—that the reading also has to do with words written down as a private act, now being made public, an act that requires time and care and love.

*

An essay seeks to tell. A poem seeks to, in Frost's words, "tell how it can," all emphasis on the "how." An essayist must get to the point; the poet must avoid getting to the point, leaving the point to the reader. The essay is a statement; the poem is a riddle.

*

Except that essays are often poetic, and poems, essay-like. Though the prevailing aesthetic insists that poems should show rather than tell and above all avoid the didactic, we have the great poetry of Whitman and the Psalms to prove that poems may also declare and instruct. We poets must be careful, given our obligation to pass on to our fellow humans whatever vision we have, not to let the prevailing aesthetic take our voices away and reduce our poetry to fragments.

*

At the academic gathering, I relearn that the academic most wants to take things apart; I, on the other hand, want to put things together—prefer my frog alive rather than dissected. In presentation after presentation, we are proudly offered pieces of the frog. Applause follows. Nobody mentions the stink.

*

In the creative writing class as it is too often taught, the instructor abdicates his role as authority and guide, either because he does not know how to say what works in student writing, or because he doesn't have the will to deal with student egos. The subject shifts from what is effective and what isn't to what feelings the author had when writing it, and what similar feelings the class can "share." Sharing by all members, including the abdicating professor, is at a premium, as it is in the counseling group, this class's true model. And in an age when personal feeling and sincerity make us all, from movie star to president, authentic, the students take it for granted they're doing real work.

*

In a letter, John Keats likens the schoolroom to life's circumstances, adding that the hornbook of the schoolroom is the heart—and that learning to read that hornbook, we develop our souls. This was before the schoolroom came to be known by poets as the workshop.

*

During the afternoon before his reading on campus, I try this proposition on William Stafford: that American poets today tend to work on the model of the creative writing seminar, conducting workshops through the mail by sending their poems to poet friends who send the poems back with suggested revisions. Check the acknowledgments page of the standard collection today, I tell him, and you'll find who the seminar members are, adding that my friend Jane Kenyon jokingly calls her group "The Committee."

The whole idea flabbergasts Stafford. "Not even my wife makes suggestions about my work," he says. Later on, he comes back to the subject, asking what other "committees" I know of, and who is on my own committee. By the end of his visit, The Committee has taken on a Bolshevik connotation, the sense of an institution out to subvert and control poetry itself. When I defend what seems to me the reasonable practice of testing new work out on friends, Stafford only replies, "We live in an occupied country."

Stafford repeats the remark when the name of a certain well-known poet and judge of poetry contests comes up in our conversation. He likens the poet-judge to a fish inspector, expert in determining which fish should be kept as they pass before him and which should be tossed aside. The trouble is, he adds, that something might pass that's well worth keeping—just isn't a fish.

*

Straightforward in his response to The Committee, Stafford is more often, like his poems themselves, oblique. In the two-and-a-half days that I host him between Maine readings, he seldom answers a question directly, preferring indirection; so he responds with another question, or with an anecdote (like his story about the fish inspector), or by quoting what someone else once said when asked a question similar to my own. Critics liken Stafford to Frost, meaning he also writes "popular" poetry. I'd liken him to Frost in the conditional way he writes and talks, never quite telling you where he stands, or all he means.

*

Someone once remarked that what drives every piece of writing is a question. The difficulty for the poet is how not quite to answer the question, placing it in the mind of the reader.

*

Poetry is the art of disclosure. As the poem moves, it must not only reveal but conceal, saving itself for its final unfolding, which must also give the sense of things withheld. In this process, the timing of image and awareness is essential. Nothing must be disclosed too soon or too late.

*

The poem must have something fast and something slow.

*

In an age when awards for achievement are handed out to brand-new writers left and right, it is important to remember that the writer of true work builds slowly. He will be lucky if one day, long after the awards are handed out, a certain mist clears, and observers notice a building all intact, where there had not been one before.

*

Though his small size may make us overlook him, the rat, Emily Dickinson shows in poem #1356, has great power precisely *because* he is "concise" and "reticent," and so he can set up housekeeping wherever he wants to without the need to pay rent, having his thoughts—his "schemes"—all to himself. Dickinson's rat is of course a version of herself, the poet who made her writing life apart from the literary establishment through concise and reticent and very powerful poems. The rat also reminds me of Linda Pastan, whose poems I read in quantity before hosting her here. Given the noise and the big gestures of her generation of American poets, you might not notice her at first, off by herself, intent on the schemes of her verse. And then you discover what she's written—poems which, though they may lack Dickinson's range of language and grammar, are similarly small, with their own power to overwhelm.

*

The novelist is a carpenter. His gift is seen in the dimensions of his creation. To appreciate what he has done, we must stand back.

The poet is a jeweler, whose gift is in smallness. To appreciate his creation, the work of a magnified eye, we must look closely.

*

The process of poems is braille-like, allowing the reader entry by touch, so that what forms in the mind and heart forms first in the hand. In writing a poem, we must find the right thing—familiar and yet mysterious to the touch—to place in the reader's hand.

*

Philip Levine does not shake your hand so much as press it, as if to place a token in it, something between the two of you that you may take away and, later on, ponder the meaning of. Straightforward and even blunt in his speech, he is at the same time tender and interior. It is a manner I come to associate with the poems from *What Work Is,* which he reads from during his visit here—poems that are direct, just as the poems of *Not This Pig* were, but that replace the muscular assertion of his earlier work with a tone that is delicate and interrogative.

How deep in Levine is the narrative impulse. He himself speaks about it on the way to a discussion with students, drawing a contrast between himself and Charles Wright, who was astonished to discover the older poet "thought in stories" since he, Wright, didn't even dream in stories. I start the discussion by asking Levine if he has any advice for student writers, and he begins a long narrative about his development as a writer and poet at Wayne University in Detroit and afterward, finishing by summarizing the story's lessons. Levine's storytelling includes dirty jokes, one of which he tells me at our final lunch with the timing of a master.

*

Apart from what I must have learned about storytelling from the dirty jokes I first told as an adolescent—the arrangement of details, the timing of the narration—I learned, I see now, how to "speak American" from them. There is a vernacular roughness in the telling that embodies the age-old American irreverence toward polite society. Also, since dirty jokes are meant to be shared apart from polite society, there's a subversiveness in the language, and a delight in the subversiveness. Yet there's a delicacy, too, a way the teller must have of taking the reader into his confidence for the private moment in which the joke is shared.

All of these ways of speaking are helpful in the creation of an American voice.

The dirty joke also gave me—and I'm sure many others—the first exposure to surrealism: the man who had his penis lengthened by the addition of a baby elephant's trunk, and was embarrassed at the cocktail party when the hostess passed out peanuts. After such jokes, Magritte seems tame.

*

So here is Randy the small engines man trying to tell me how to troubleshoot my failed lawn tractor over the phone. Never mind that the steps he gives are hard to follow and even out of order. Listen to the accent and rhythm of his speech, rehearsed for this conversation all his life; here is the true order, in which there is not one mistake. Forget how he is supposed to say it and listen to how he says it.

*

Lore Segal, on our campus as a Woodrow Wilson Writing Fellow, tells me about her graduate student who claims free verse is a hoax—its line breaks, which have replaced rhyme, merely arbitrary. Yet line breaks are the most natural thing in the world. In fact, when we speak thoughtfully about things that matter to us, we all use them. Thinking the sentence, as one does in free verse, requires it. When we hear someone who does not speak in line breaks or does so in a programmatic way, we know we are listening to a commercial or a political speech, and we suspect lying. So the line breaks of spoken language also have to do with telling the truth.

Shaping the free verse poem, then, we imitate the process of thoughtful and truthful conversation, our line breaks indicating the stresses of our meditation as we say our sentences.

*

What is in that space the sentence of the free verse poem takes into itself as it goes down the page from line to line, becoming more poetic as it moves? It is a wordlessness which the lines touch against and make expressive, claiming it, too, as part of the poem. It is also the image of thought itself as it snaps from one line to the next, so as the poem moves we glimpse at the edge of the right margin the mind at work making the poem.

*

Maxine Kumin, a witty concluder of poems, writes that the most satisfactory ending in a poem resembles a bolt sliding into the door latch. Still, I prefer my door just ajar.

*

At the conclusion of a poem he wrote after the moon landing in the late 1960's, Philip Booth implored Americans to "come to your senses." In the electronic nineties, as we continue to deify technological advances and the mechanical understanding they represent, Booth's words should appear on banners in every city and town. Now as always, the true knowledge is the knowledge of the heart, and true human advancement results from events as small as the lightness a poet might feel on discovering a new way of thinking and feeling. No one will ever televise such an event, nor will it deposit a man on the moon. But it may help us to come to our senses.

*

Reading Gerald Stern's *Selected Poems* before his appearance on campus, I find those few beautifully complete poems on which his reputation mainly rests. Most of them are about animals victimized by technology, through which he reflects on the affliction of our own animal selves, so dominated by the civilization we have made that we can't hear their cries. Of these poems, "The Dog" is the most wonderful. Then there are his poems about the city, which reveal again the suffering of the deeper self (the instinctual, intuitive, sniffing, howling core of us), overwhelmed by the technology of the metropolis. Oh, the blasted cityscapes of Stern, their sorrow!

*

I spend time with Charles Simic before my reading for graduate students at the University of New Hampshire and rediscover his splendid humor, the humor of the damned, delivered out of the side of his mouth in a way that reminds me of the gangsters of old movies or the thugs of old comics. It says we are all in on the joke of Truth and Justice, and happy as a result to be outlaws in a club of outlaws. In his company I am a thug poet, pleased to be in the gang whose boss is Simic, and whose truth is poetry.

*

"Unconscious," my fifth- and sixth-grade teachers called me, and the two of them once fell into step behind me as I walked home for lunch to taunt me with the word. At home, my mother named me "Stubborn." Yet it was only by being both of these things that I became a poet.

*

A friend asks, partly in fun, "If you could change something that happened in your life, what would it be?" It occurs to me to say, surprising even myself with my seriousness, that because my life has given me the only materials I have as a poet, my objective must not be to change my life, but to accept it exactly as I have lived it.

*

Yet accepting what his life has brought is difficult for Donald Hall. I sit with him three months after Jane Kenyon's death at a memorial reading for her in the Frost barn in Derry, New Hampshire. As others read her poems, he sometimes makes comments to himself as if no one else were there: "Ah, Gus!" he says aloud, listening to her description of their dog. At the end of the event, he stands and tells the audience about the volume he and Jane worked on from February until her death—the book called *Otherwise*. Then, in this period he calls "the long day of three months," he takes up the manuscript of that book to read the new poems, his voice unsteady on the occasional passage that refers to him. Reading from that black notebook, his hair uncut and tangled, his feelings tangled, too, he sustains himself for one more hour, the two of them still together in poetry.

*

For the writer and the reader, poetry is dangerous. It asks that we be connected with our feelings, and it asks that we try to be whole, against every impulse to compartmentalize and deny.

*

The wholeness poetry seeks is also dangerous to the classroom as we seem to have it—a place that defines intelligence according to the ability to rehearse and perform left-brain skills, like the sad schoolroom Philip Levine describes in his poem "Milkweed," where students experience

> the long day
> after day of the History of History
> or the tables of numbers and order
> as the clock slowly [pays] out the moments.

Given his education in such a place, it's no wonder that at the conclusion of this poem Levine's narrator ends up walking "the empty woods, bent over, / crunching through oak leaves." But then "a froth of seeds" from a milkweed drifts by, engaging his memory and his heart, reminding him of the childhood world he knew before school stamped the life out of it. The difficult and subversive challenge for teachers of poetry and poetry writing is to find a spot indoors, among numbers, order and the clock, where such seeds might grow.

Alive in His Trousers

We were crazy in love. Crazy. He wasn't handsome. He was maybe even ugly. Abraham Lincoln ugly. With face bumps like Abe had. But he had angel radiance. He outdid the sun. His very glance polished you. He rubbed light into your skin as if light were lotion. I loved him. Nothing with this much promise ever happened to me is what I thought when Al and I started up together. I was wrong, about the promise. The feelings that the promise gave rise to, though, they honest to God were that first green, snub-nosed crocus push out of dirty, hard-packed February snow. They were Lazarus feelings, rising, rising, rising from the beetle-chewed quiet dead. I'll go one step further: they were Easter-Sunday-roll-away-the-stone feelings.

He was poplar-tree tall. Rib-counting skinny. Stripped down to his baggy Jockey shorts, he looked like an El Greco Christ who wandered off canvas. He had that elongated, starved, gaunt blue boniness that makes you feel so sad first in your heart and then, clunk, deep in your stomach, as if you swallowed a big rock washed smooth by rivers. Sometimes when we got naked, I studied his kneecaps and wide pelvis and thought I'd die of grief to see bone poke up so close to skin. I touched him and thought about lustrous white soup bones I saw at the butcher shop.

Believe me, if I ever fall in love again, I won't fall in love with a thin man. I'll try a fat man. Fat men forgive more. Al couldn't forgive himself for loving me, and I think now that he never forgave me for being around to love. He never said, "Polly, I won't ever forgive you." But I think he didn't. I think he won't. But that's another, different story than the one I'm telling here.

Al's face was narrow, nose long and pinched at the nostrils, lips no more than two pink lines. He was Norwegian, on both sides. His eyes were Norse bright blue. By the time we met, he was in his early fifties. He wore rimless bifocals. The prescription was strong; when I, longing to see the world as Al saw the world, set his glasses on my nose, whatever I tried to look at blurred. His blond hair had thinned and streaked gray. His skin had seamed and wrinkled. He walked jerkily, the way a marionette will in amateur hands. He had big bony schoolboy wrists and long wide feet. His toes bunched up on top of each other, and he had bunions from wearing shoes that were too tight. "A peasant's feet," he called them.

I used to think about Al's penis alive in his trousers, as if his penis were the hero in a novel. "Big Al" was the name I gave his hero-penis, and I liked to work up long *bildungsroman*, *Augie March*-type adventures for Big Al. I'd mix stories he'd told me with details I guessed at. I'd set him to thinking, interior-monologue style, about the first time he spurted into a handkerchief. I'd have him be twelve, at the North Dakota crippled children's school where his parents worked as doctor and chief matron. He'd be alone in one of the school's twelve infirmary beds. He'd be getting over pneumonia (which he had three times) and violently attracted to the nurse who'd bathed away his fever sweats. I'd get a face for the nurse, blond curls and round high breasts bursting her white uniform. I'd sketch out the rough infirmary sheets and the view out the window to green grass and morning sunshine. I'd figure cotton pajamas for him, the kind that tie at the waist with a cord. I'd get twelve-year-old Al's fingers creeping down under the waistband, across his warm, hairless boy tummy, his fingers making their way toward the still-juvenile Big Al, who up to that moment had only known the frustration of one-after-another boyish boners. Another day, I'd add ten years to Big Al's age, turn him twenty-two and roguish, his circumcised head bright pink. I'd bring in the chesty brunette farmer's daughter who Al had told me had flirted with him during the summer between his junior and senior college years. Al bucked hay that summer. Big Al was all for this brunette and pressed against his owner's Levi's on evenings when Al and the brunette took hand-in-hand walks through her father's apple orchard and kissed under branches heavy with apples that needed another month before ripening. Several times the brunette started to go for the buttons on Al's Levi's. She wanted to get at Big Al. I'd turn myself into the brunette. I conjured her frustration, the rocky ache low in her stomach. Al told me this flirtation with the farmer's daughter never went anywhere. "I was scared," he said, "that she might have VD."

Once we were through making love, Al would do something that really annoyed me. He would get up out of bed and go wash off Big Al, as if he were dirty because he'd been down in me. Big Al was so long that he hung down in the sink. Al scrubbed the big guy as if he weren't even attached to him, as if he were some grease-caked kitchen utensil.

I loved Al, I think now, more than I liked him.

The Nudes

"Come look at the nudes, Carla." My uncle started heading towards his studio with his Chihuahua slung over his shoulder, the dog's ass snug in his fat hand. I skipped behind him, happy, cracking spearmint gum. Uncle Samson breathed with a chronic stuffy nose and dragged the heels of his feet as he walked because he didn't have the energy or interest for either function.

"Wow," I said. I was in a sunny jungle of nudes dipped in oily color. Naked women with big brown nipples were coming at me from all directions. The unframed canvases hung in horizontal rows in a semicircle around the room like double rows of uneven teeth in a shark's mouth. Some sat very high on the walls, some low. One painting sat on an easel with a cream-colored shroud over it.

"How do you like them, Carla?" Uncle Sam shifted Teddy to the other shoulder.

"I like that one, Uncle Sam." The fumes made me careless, but I made it over to the wet canvas of the brunette nude in turquoise water up to her thighs without tripping on cans of turpentine or slipping on plastic wrappers that coated Uncle Sam's fresh Cuban cigars. "This water—it's not the same color as out back."

Uncle Samson and Aunt Henrietta lived on the harbor. At night the water looked black, and occasionally I could see a water rat's glistening back skimming the surface. There was always a slight smell of salt and fish, but the only fish I ever saw so close to their house were the small minnows I caught with glass milk bottles and string right off the dock. You had to use Uncle Samson's boat, *Gone Wild*, to get to the striped bass and flounder out near Scotch Caps, the rocky area seven miles out into the Long Island Sound.

Uncle Samson rested his gooey cigar stub on the windowsill and sat down on the bench splattered with all the stunning colors that surrounded his women. Teddy got bored if he wasn't being rubbed and left the studio looking for Aunt Hen's poodle. The toy-sized dog could always be found licking her own genitalia at the foot of Aunt Hen's bed.

"Curla." Uncle Sam looked serious, the way he looked when we fished off the boat. He'd pick up the slack from his rod by instinct and just stare out on the water's surface. Waiting. I figured he shared my hopes of seeing a sleek gray fin there.

He said it again, "Curla." I never corrected his pronunciation as I would have if he were another ten-year-old. Besides, he put a spin on all his words.

Uncle Sam lowered the music on the stereo with the most gentle fingering. He had a soft touch so it was hard for me to picture him as a boxer, but that was a long time ago, like he said. The song was familiar to me since he played it over and over while he painted with the door closed, *"Bella Maria de mi Alma"* ("Beautiful Maria of My Soul"). Then he leaned over his belly as far as he could and said without breath, "Curla...the nudes...they love to dance."

My parents were smooth dancers so I was familiar with all the actions this secret implied. Mom and Dad were elegantly romantic when they danced. They exchanged looks while they glided around, looks inspired by each other. I glanced at the nudes with thick feet.

"You mean they rumba—in there?" I wondered if they had enough room. I imagined them tumbling out of their square of canvas.

Uncle Sam got up slowly, eyeing the room for his cigar stub. He was wearing his cherry-colored bathing trunks with a terry-cloth robe draped over his shoulders. The ends of his belt dragged on the floor, he never tied anything.

"Where's Mother?" Mother was a name he called Aunt Hen. Uncle Sam was forever adjusting the windows so his studio could be filled with that southeast breeze off the harbor.

"She's on the patio with Mom and Dad. They're waiting for the fireworks. You can see 'em perfect from there."

Uncle Sam left me alone with the nudes. Most canvases held three or four women doing water ballet in a lime-green pond, or stepping out of the water linking arms with other nudes. Two black-haired ladies faced each other in a cha-cha. Some were lounging by the grassy areas near the tropical water. A few held hands in a circle under a tree. The women looked up in a cobalt blue sky or shyly down. Their mouths were full and shocking pink. They were satisfied from the easy rhythms of their day. I could smell the flowers and mossy waters that were love seats for their bodies. One lady sat on a rock, her legs crossed, and stared at me. I knocked down a small tower of beer cans as I left the studio.

A burst of fireworks started falling slowly over the black harbor. You had to walk through Aunt Hen's living room to get to just about anywhere in the sprawling house. The picture window acted like a frame for the harbor and the patio where Aunt Hen, Uncle Sam, and my parents sat with multicolored Japanese lights strung over their heads. I could hear Aunt Hen's muffled voice from my hiding place in the living room, "Jesus Christ, Sammy!" The white poodle was in her lap, busy licking herself while Aunt Hen quickly drank her highball.

From my spot behind a massive jardiniere I felt well protected from the powers in my aunt's home. Buddhas and stiff geishas proved to me you can't trust everyone in this world. All the beings here had glass eyes that followed me, even when I wasn't paying attention to them. Two Asian cats the size of German shepherds sat on each side of the china cabinet—Tom Shue's cats. Once while I played possum in the back of our car, my mom whispered to my dad, "Those Asian cats—aren't they stunning?—were a gift to Hen from that shady character, Tom Shue."

Aunt Hen kept a drawer for good girls in my favorite table, an end table standing on bird-claw legs. Inside was a copy of *The Story of Little Black Sambo,* who tried to escape the mouths of tigers by giving them his beautiful clothes. There were several trinkets from Singapore, and two porcelain mockingbirds. There was an old postcard from Fiji stuck in the back of the drawer. I yanked it out and read Tom Shue's faded signature. The note smelled spicy, and I laughed when I read the closing, "Of course, my sweet and angelic Hen, I will be forever yours."

Over this end table was a rather small painting of a nude. She was different than the others in the studio. Shy maybe. A teenager? She was wet, her shiny hair dripping into a V in the middle of her back. I could see her profile, a flat nose, a full face. She was wrapping a towel around her buttocks with one leg propped up on the edge of something. I never noticed her before because a handsome Great White sat on the end table beneath her, his muscular tail bent upwards.

The screen door slapped shut, and I heard my father's footsteps looking for me. I was relieved to hear his voice. "Carla—you wanna miss the finale?" I could see the top of the dripping colors from my spot but agreed to go outside with the adults. "Dad, I'll be out in a minute. I have to get my fishing bottles ready for the morning"—cementing the fact that I would be spending the night there without my parents. I left my musty corner behind the jardiniere and joined the others on the patio.

Uncle Samson explained to Teddy why the finale was "a Jackson Pollock splash." The smell of sulphur and gin was a little too much. After my father urged me outside, he wasn't even looking at the display. I climbed on my father's lap even though I was just about too big for this sort of thing and whispered, "Dad! The noise—it will scare the fish!" My heart broke thinking of all the plump silvery bass swimming away to other waters. Uncle Sam said, "Curla, how do you like the fireworks?" Aunt Hen's poodle kept yapping and quieted down only to kiss Aunt Hen under the chin with about ten licks in a row. "Sammy, get Johnny another drink here!" I followed Uncle Sam back into the house to assist him in making a cocktail for my father.

I grabbed the mermaid ice thong and filled the glasses with ice. "Uncle Sam, the nudes, they like fishing?" I had to make sure he was planning to take me out on the boat in the morning. I could take one of the smaller portraits—the shy one—and tie her to the seat in the cabin. He could have a sandwich with her, if he wanted to. The ladies were my insurance.

"No, Curla." He dropped the cherries in the highballs. He was still wearing his trunks and robe, while everyone else was dressed. "No, the girls must be home. And, they need me first thing in the morning."

"For what?"

"Who would hold their towels for them after they bathe?"

I couldn't think of one other person who could do this job for the nudes. I started to panic thinking of our schedule for the morning—I prayed that their bathtime would be over before the tide started to go out.

We served the drinks on the patio, and my mother was giving

my father a "that's enough" look. My father was egging on his cousin, as usual, getting her worked up about the stock market and real estate values where Aunt Hen made most of her money. She owned several buildings in town, one of them was a showroom for Chryslers. Uncle Sam's job was to schmooze with customers, a job that Aunt Hen said was one that he was good for. Once he hung a blond nude with a pink lei around her head like a crown in the showroom over a salesman's desk, but Aunt Hen ordered it off the wall.

Uncle Sam was serving my mother with his best manners, and I was trying to prevent my mother from thinking about me going out on the boat in the morning. Mom never learned to swim or bait a hook.

"Sammy!" Aunt Hen bounced up a bit from her seat.

"Yes, Mother." Uncle Sam bit the start of his cigar whenever Aunt Hen was about to reprimand him.

"There's no gas in the tanks, for God's sake. You're not even going to make it to the fuel dock!"

Uncle Sam watched the last explosion in the sky. "Don't worry, Mother, I'll make it."

"Jesus Christ. You should spend less time with those goddamn paint brushes and pay more attention to what needs to be done around here." Aunt Hen shooed the poodle off her lap.

My mother butted in, unintentionally changing the subject. "There are plenty of fish right here for Carla to catch, Sam. Don't worry about getting gas. Plenty for her to do right here."

"Mom, did you bring the Wonder bread for the milk bottles?"

Fishing for minnows was depressing compared to being out on the open Sound. While I sat on the dock and stuffed bits of bread down the neck of the bottle, I always had one eye on the rocky wall that separated the harbor from the grounds of the house. Sporadically, rats ran in and out of familiar routes. Every time I ran up or down the wooden stairway that leaned against this rocky maze, I feared that one of them would nip my feet with its pin teeth. When Tom Shue visited, wearing a white suit, he made cooing noises to the rats the way Uncle Sam coaxed Teddy on his lap, but the rats never came to him.

The fireworks were through, and the sky was quiet. The audience of boats and dinghies started to rev up their motors and left their spots in a disorderly parade. Mom and Dad were starting their goodbyes. I was relieved to see my mother go before she jeopardized my early morning trip on *Gone Wild*. She pushed brown strings from my face and said, "You be good. I left the bread on the kitchen counter." I hugged my father's waist good night.

As I tried to fall asleep that night in the guest bedroom, I was thinking about being out on the water. It was the best feeling I had ever had. I easily jumped from the boat's upper deck to the dock and pushed us off before jumping right back on again. Uncle Sam would steer until we got out of the harbor. The best feeling started every time we left the dock and I watched the house get smaller and smaller and smaller. When the cold spray of the wake hit my face, I knew I was free.

On the way out to Scotch Caps, after Uncle Sam passed the five-mile-per-hour markers, he would hold up his hand as a sign and yell back to me, "Hold on, Curla, I'm gonna pick her up!" Usually, we passed the regulars—*Innisfree, Old Suzanne,* and, if Uncle Sam was having a lucky day, *Little Women.* Uncle Sam never reprimanded me, he never even tried to tell me what to do. Our jobs were cut out for us, and we worked silently with each other. We'd anchor and bait, fix the lures if necessary, and, once in a while, exchange a dream.

"Uncle Sam? How far do you think she can go?" I asked him one day. I rubbed the teak inlays near the steering wheel as if the boat was a horse.

"As long as she can sniff her way between the rocks and keep her tail out of the mud, she can go anywhere her heart desires."

"And, as long as she has plenty of juice in the engine."

His tan face wrinkled into a frown, then he smiled without turning in my direction. You couldn't hang around Aunt Hen without being influenced by her one way or the other.

"How about Montauk?" I unsnapped a beer for him.

"What are you dancin' around, Curla?"

"Tigers, makos...I'd even pull in a nurse. I'm not fussy."

Uncle Sam never budged. He just stared out. I didn't even push him, and he asked, "Got the stomach for chum?"

"Me?" I was game. He knew I was game. I could make a hook

look like a bulky Christmas stocking the way I inserted the thing perfectly through the center of a sandworm's entire body.

When we drove back from Scotch Caps that day, Uncle Sam was thinking. He must have been charting out a route to the tip of Long Island where the ocean warmed up by the end of August. He was probably thinking of the best way to avoid those clumps of rock beneath the water that could rip your boat apart if you didn't know enough to avoid them. We'd pass Port Washington and Greenport and by the time we reached Shelter Island, we'd probably stop at one of those Dock 'n' Dine places. Finally, he'd get me to the ocean with real fish, the kind that circled their prey.

I was lost in my thoughts, too. I wanted to run through my future to the day when I would be standing on the bloody fishing docks in Montauk next to a heap of dead sharks.

The next morning I was the first one to get up and sat in the kitchen dressed for fishing. There was a naked girl hanging on the wall over the pine table. She was sitting down on a bench with her back facing me, but she managed to look over her shoulder. There was a basket of odd shaped apples next to her.

Uncle Sam joined me for breakfast. He had his terry-cloth robe on, and his hair was wet. His face flushed as he searched for fruit in the refrigerator and found a mango that was already peeled.

"Everyone have their bath, Uncle Sam?" I was hopeful that his services for the nudes were over and done with and that we could get on with our day's activities.

I recognized the sounds of Aunt Hen's Italian bracelets so I was prepared for her entrance. She came rushing into the kitchen with her full-length satin robe on. A Japanese maple tree sprang from the bottom of the robe and fanned out across her broad shoulders.

"Sammy, Carla will wait here with me while you go to the fuel dock—and have them check that motor again!"

Uncle Sam left the kitchen without any comment, and I was hoping he wasn't going to close himself in his studio, because if he did we'd never make it out to Scotch Caps before the tide went out.

I suggested to Aunt Hen that I was going to remind him about getting to Rosie's Bait and Tackle Shop for the sandworms. Rosie always had just one box of sandworms left in her fridge every time we went to buy them.

Aunt Hen drank her tea standing up and said, "Honey, I think his boxing days have taken their toll on Uncle Sammy. He can't breathe right from taking punches, but it's his brain that's stuffed up."

It sounded like she added, "That chooch."

After I knocked on the door several times, Uncle Sam and Teddy let me in the studio.

"*Quiéreme mucho*" ("How Much Do You Want Me?") was playing too loud for my ears. He had Teddy on his left shoulder while he rubbed some finishing touches on the nude that had been under a shroud last night.

Teddy squirmed down to the floor and tested me for a rub, but I was concerned about the tide. I could feel a nice strong wind even in the studio.

"Uncle Sam?"

His thumb and forefinger were coated in pinks and flesh tones. He didn't have his painting clothes on, but he wiped his hands on his sides anyway.

I picked up an old rag with turps and dark paint on it and offered it to him. "Don't you think we better get going? I mean, it's getting late and the last time we got out to Scotch Caps I said we were lucky with all the bites and you said that timing was everything."

"Bull's-eye, little Curl." He didn't take his eyes off his work-in-progress. "See her? She's just about to show me her charms." He stood back and admired this one. "Let me finish up, Curla, then I'll change for the trip."

I walked back through the living room to the kitchen and stopped to look at Tom Shue's cats since the morning light gave me a different outlook on things. I heard Aunt Hen's teacup hit the saucer every once in a while, and I figured I might as well get her going about Tom Shue to get her mind off lazy Uncle Sam—but she wasn't the type of lady to forget anything.

"Tommy Shue?" She put her teacup in the sink like she was fed up with it. She lowered her voice, and it startled me as much as if she had screamed. "Honey, all men are the same—with the exception of my Tommy."

Just the sight of me in my fishing gear must have reminded her about the gas, and I could see her pale cheeks come to life with anger. Uncle Sam told me repeatedly while teaching me to troll that his wife was full of piss and vinegar.

I picked up the teacup to distract her and held it in front of my face. She grabbed it from me and said, "No, honey, put it up to the sunlight." She held the teacup high in front of the sunny window and put a spoon behind it with the other hand. "Now, look, Carla, if you can see right through china—see?—you've got yourself the real thing."

It was getting hot now, and my plan to fish off the boat rather than the lousy dock out back was making me desperate. "I better get the buckets and stuff out of the shed, Aunt Hen." I was sweaty, I wanted to be out of there.

I followed the worn Persian rug through the narrow hallway to the studio on the other side of the house. When I got there I thought I was in the wrong room, but it smelled right. The door was open. The breeze was blowing the sheer curtains farther into the room, and I could hear calm waves hitting the sides of the dock. There was only one canvas on an easel in the center of the studio. Teddy sat on the floor, abandoned.

"Teddy? Where is everyone? Where are the nudes—and Uncle Sam?"

Uncle Sam was nowhere to be found. Only his robe was there; it was bunched up, dirty with oils, laying on the splattered bench. I could smell fresh paint and the yellowy linseed oil he always worked with.

I went to the open window and looked out on the boat. I didn't see any sign of Uncle Samson. Usually, just before we left for a couple of hours of fishing, he would fool with the motor and check things on board.

I wondered if my mother found out about the trip to the Caps and had nixed my fun the way she often did. I stood there too frustrated to even cry. I had even prepared sandwiches, and brought sodas and beer. I gave Teddy a rub. His eyes looked more crusty than usual.

A whiff of salt water blew in, reminding me that had I been on the boat with Uncle Sam, my line would be cast and I'd be ready for a good-sized bass to come my way. There was nothing like a nice swift jerk of the line when you knew you had one. I stood in the center of the studio in front of the easel holding the one canvas left in the room. I stared at it. The oils on it were shining, and because of the glare I went up to it as close as I could. At first, all I noticed were the colors. They were muted, unlike the sharp colors and flatness of Uncle Sam's paintings. This one was amazingly different. A Florentine table was in the middle of the scene with a very large man standing on top of it. I wondered if the table might break. The man was naked, just like the women off to the sides of the picture peeking at him from behind trees. He had one leg up a little bit, he was dancing. In fact, he was in a spin. His face was a blur, but I could tell he was happy.

The Twelve Hats of Napoleon

In the painting the twelve hats look pretty much alike. Tricorns, they're called, and when studying them in their invisible grid, one inevitably thinks of his face.

An allegory about Napoleon: The parts of his face had always hated each other. Like wild stars in a burning sky, many-a-time they came dangerously close to colliding.

Nose, mouth, eyes and ears, hair and scalp—they were enemies to each other, and only I know why.

The mouth made the first move. It picked up and traveled south into the chin's territory while wind chimes tangled in a breeze.

Staring at the maps of foreign cities, he dreamed of love. Hat stuffed deep upon the mighty head. Imagine: Men dressed as women, women dressed as birds, birds eating, being eaten.

Bright colorful flags pop in the icy air.
Glory he had truly intended to share.

Then the left eye began to pitch and buck like a rowboat on a huge and moody sea. Pretty soon it became unmoored and drifted. Its gleam played moon to the entire landscape.

The nose had always been partial to extreme means, and it resorted to various so-called Acts of God—flood, eruption, and then avalanche.

All this happened in 1815.

When the shock of dark hair joined the rebellion, the great face knew that the future must be feared.

In the end one is left with little more than the desperate search for symbols—hat hanging in air, hat encrusted with snow, hat as signature, hat eroding, hatlessness.

Face it: We live for the knife storm.

Water Towers on City Buildings

There are men like these, who stand above
the loft and gloss of downtown rhetoric,
who hold for us a quiet surplus, and think—
not of present need and use—but,
of what is necessary in dire times.

There are those who go unnoticed, apart
from the general chat, who have in mind
the words we choose, yet hold them in a lonely air
where interest and meaning grow,
who wait until the time is right, and know
when what was once cheap coal
has earned its diamondhood.

Some men's lives are as co-incidental
as these water towers trapped on city buildings;
call them wooden-headed, chrome-domed, or roughed
with splinters; coarse, flat-topped, or scraggly.
They have more character than the Tin Man of Oz,
and for our purposes, brim with heart. Surely
we can learn from these: seamy barrels,
afterthoughts, these stoic ramparts
that hold water, yet mean nothing until
we're out of what we're desperate for, then turn
to those who've kept it well, and always have
been with us, unadorned, all but forgotten,
tough, loving towers.

Dear John Donne

If death is a rest stop, a sweet state
Line, where we pause in the poppies
As our souls check the map, will I be
Spared that recurring dream of youth,
The one when I rose from my warm bed,
And appeared reciting from *My Weekly Reader*
In front of the whole third grade? Will I
Hear behind me, again, Mrs. Nerthling
On her perch, sharpening those talons
While her hawk's beak burns down
The limp wick of my spine?
When I lift my eyes from the hard words
Will they meet the rapturous gaze of Cathy—
Princess, future centerfold, gown and tiara
Glittering, all her attentions garnishing
My every stuttered phrase—fourth row,
Second seat? Or will they meet the glare
Of my idiot rival Eugene, whom I wish would
Remove his feet from the back of her chair?
Will my voice again wrap around that last
Elegant syllable, and my head drop
In a subtle bow that only she can see?
Then, looking down, will my horror discover
That I'd stood there the whole time
In my electrically white Fruit of the Looms,
Size eight, with nary even a pocket
To hold the quarter I need for lunch?
Dear John, if that's what it means, a short
And dreamy sleep, look for me on the bypass
Driving straight through.

Looking for Father in My Reflection

I search the pond's portrayal of my face
for my father. This woman's brow, so smooth,
disdains its heritage and hides the truth.
Its lineaments reveal almost no trace
of his. But I must clear an open space
to mirror him in, because since his death
I feel as distant as "map-isopleth,"
which is, I've read, the term surveyors use
for borderlines. Now something in me seeks
to cross over when a face I think was him
combines with mine—a single cast—my cheeks
with whiskers. Our eyes merge across a chasm
of time and look for the pure frame our future takes
—one portrait, limned in ripple-cubism.

My Father, The Commander, Poolside at Fifty-Five

Think of him all that summer
at poolside, in seersucker shorts
a size too big
and a sombrero,
hoisting highballs—
a few past a few too many—
in memory of his Men. His "boodies."

Or floating in the pool, say, with swimfins,
his body, bird's nest frail
after surgery, the stitches running
like the Yangtze River
down his chest
Krazy Kat in all directions.

Not once but twice
when the wind blew his toupee
to the table, "I am not a failure,"
he said.

To cap it off,
a toga party
at which no one showed.
Only his bony shoulders like a boy's
in the dim light, his gaze
like a bulb suddenly gone out.

MICHAEL RYAN

A Version of Happiness

for Ellen Bryant Voigt

Tonight the band's Nigerian—
Afro-Cuban, last week; next week, Cajun:
the summer multicultural concert series
in the San Juan Capistrano Library courtyard;
two hundred of us, all ages, in the audience;
Edenic evening air and stars: tickets six bucks.
You'd love this music, this place:
the musicians are like poets (they have day jobs)
and they're *good:* they play this music
because they love it, love making it,
love being able to make it—together
(unlike poets?). The sound
each is part of and takes part in
feeds back through their collective body
for the next chord and phrase—
into fingers, lips, lungs, even elbows
in the case of the maniac god on the congas
when the guitars and horns cease
and the lead singers politely step aside
that we may witness his five-minute solo
and feel, as they do, the triumph of prowess
over human clumsiness, and notice
who's drumming us into this happy trance.
Now they give us this chance: to notice.
They eye us like parents watching children
unwrap gifts. He sweats not only for us
but for what against all reason he can do
with whapping palms and shuttling elbows
that have multiplied exponentially beyond his allotted
two of each, because how can one man do this?
Ancient our amazement and this power
that has caused sane men to run point-blank into fusillades

176

or shuttle themselves, their wives, and their post-marital
extra twenty pounds behind a column of the courtyard portico
to dance beside an eleven-year-old with her mother
in probably the girl's last summer as a child.
All evening these two have been a joy to notice:
the girl goofing with her dancing, freckled, gangly,
her impossibly sweet grin enhanced by the obligatory missing tooth,
her mom I imagine still her best friend
before the teenage hormonal tsunami sweeps her away
like a beach shack. Mom's late thirtyish,
bespectacled, frumpy, doing dorky disco moves (like me)
she probably learned riding *her* tsunami
in front of a mirror to BeeGees songs
with an inconsolable crush on John Travolta
and no clue that happiness
might come someday from a parental talent for pleasure
in what another can do.
Your father thought your playing piano for the choir
in Baptist churches in rural Virginia
the pinnacle of achievement.
He loved music that much but couldn't play it,
so he wanted you to, and you did.
How deep child-love is. I guess
we'll do anything to make our parents love us
even if they can't. The ones who can,
though—it's ludicrous for me
to try to distill in words what it does to be loved
like that, but surely it's visible
in you, my dear friend. This frumpy mom
shows it, too, as does this girl
despite disasters, trials, and heartbreaks
she may have already and certainly will suffer.
Nobody gets out alive, except in spirit
(the lucky ones), and I feel lucky
to have you to write to about this,
and to have this now, in time—this music
which couldn't be more bodily
but translates beautifully.

Solace

Having awakened again at 4 a.m.
inside the skull-dungeon in which my brain's chained
like a nasty old man
muttering, nattering, keeping me from sleeping
with the usual complaints about the accommodations,
I focused as usual on my breathing,
asked blessings on every living human being
by name, alphabetically, one at a time,
except of course two or three book reviewers
and those responsible for "entertainment news,"
yellow smiley-face stickers, celebrities
who own eight or more Porsches, and checkout clerks
named Staci saying, "Have a great day!,"
gave up, got up, and was being lowered gently
into quiescence by reading good writing
when slambangclang a garbage can outside
upended. Yogis spend lifetimes
clearing consciousness enough
that the body, as if literally weighted
by thought, might levitate a quarter-inch,
whereas I shot to the ceiling in a nanosecond,
hovering like a tenth-ton hummingbird
until brain-man informed me dryly
what was outside wasn't human.
I killed my reading lamp and shone a flashlight
through the window: a cartoon raccoon
dissecting my actual trash bags with her
dexterous, delicate, spidery claws.
Tell me this animal is not intelligent.
She had climbed onto the garbage can
and rocked it to knock it down.
About me and my flashlight beam
she was utterly incurious.
I wish I were so fearless.
For five minutes of our lives

I got to watch her eat some chicken bones
(I thought I cleaned pretty well myself
three days ago), flipping them
like batons to gnaw the ungnawed ends:
neither enduring peace of mind nor revelation
nor strung-out crackhead with a zip gun,
but an earthly privilege, gratis,
despite the mess she left for me
that to her is food.

NATASHA SAJÉ

A Minor Riot at the Mint

Custome is the most certain Mistresse of language, as the
publicke stampe makes current money. But we must not
be too frequent with the mint, every day coyning.
—Ben Jonson

Into my pocket slips a folded note, creased
like labia, cached with private promise.
Pea blossoms in broth. And my *in petto*
pleasure in thinking the missive
for me, the edges keen against
my thumb, my plotting to be alone and open it.
Is it tame as a Hepplewhite chair
or as nubile as a pitchfork?

The ship rolls through open water,
dirty in the bay around Rio.
I'm a crazy sailor on the gravy boat,
a woman of means. This letter's mine only
till St. Geoffrey's Day, and if
the paper degrades, that's how it goes
with money. I'll wave the wealth
where any frigate bird can snatch it.

O my mackintosh,
my bilbo, my cistern, my confiture,

I love you so much you breathe me away.

FAITH SHEARIN

Alone

When I was younger I loved until I disappeared.
I rested my head in my hand and saw only
the beloved: his unruly words, the chocolate
of his eyes, each hair on his head a vine

from the soul. If we were sitting at a table—
the other people around us, the table itself,
the light and sound of the place where we ate,
my own hand, even my breathing

melted away. Alone in my bedroom,
I often felt love a second time. I pressed my palm
to my ribs and fingered my heart. Sometimes
my body was as foreign as a stranger's.

I filled the silence of sheets and pillows
with myself. My thoughts, the weight of
my hair in my hand: the room was colored
by this. It has taken me all these years to feel

myself and another at the same time. Even so,
a fascinating speaker at a cocktail party
will narrow my range of vision. My husband's
face against a pillow has caused whole rooms to collapse.

EVA SKRANDE

Animal Empire

Peacock, I have to tell you,
your feathers are beautiful. Snake,
your length is my life.
Mighty elephant, I never forget
the corner I came from.
Your shell, long-living turtle, is my crown.
I preach the laugh of the hyena.
Dear horse, thank you for my head
of hair. Thank you, sweet ox,
for the strength of roses. Whale, teach me
how to keep warm for centuries.
Yes, I am hard. My skin,
faithful alligator, has roughened
(though the dove has blessed my right hand)
so I can roam all over the earth,
looking for the lucky life
promised to me by the antelope,
for the deer that promised to marry me,
the gazelle that loaned me its leap,
the king who loaned me his breath.

BRUCE SMITH

Jelly 292

"I will smash their guitar."
—Joan Miró

The force that drives the left-handed guitarist
    Waking from a dream that again escapes me
to play right-handed... immortality, frets
    like the eyes of vermin. No sheep fold, no birth
chords and stops, scorings, the music itself
    lava, breasts, no color or the rogue, once a woman
herself, himself impels him toward the cold
    flashes through. I remember only *89 cents,* a dream
of the right arm, tied up, smacked, he used
    of the expense of a decade without remembering
a surgical tube in his teeth and the works
    the feeling or the fiction. There's some contention
the white horse an engine that rode him out
    it's coming back to me now, some cake
of paradise and the fluent modes of bar beat
    eaten like the placenta of the dead baby
and rags into the family plot and lawsuits.
    and the bitter foreign tongue of love
The harm is the music. Its tactic is loss
    89 cents, odd, something minus something
his name is legion. The taste is elastic,
    like a tag on some merchandise
vulcanized rubber—everything he sang expelled what
    it could be sense as in sensation, intuition
can again injure him—the demon life
    meaning, judgment, the functions of touch
of a lover: bubbles of mud and sulfur from the volcano burst
    as scents: the smell, the nose as Scheherazade
scorch, then another desire axe-madness, rut and
    ripping away almost one hundred veils to avoid

tax, infra-dig, loss of face . . .
   what I might find: desire costs
I might as well go back yonder across the hill
   the dream's dice and labor
Because if my baby don't love me
   change for a dollar
I know her sister will

Letter to T.

Spring rain. Inklings, earthlings, wet present
   The sequence of events, that's what's best, when the clots
participles and shivers before red sun and cicadas
   dissolve as from the drugs...
or in your city, Santoria, snow cones, dubbed syllables
   to hear the names, to have the characters cast down
The patients at the hospital believe the *Ching*
   their lives each time and die, dye in the wool
before they believe darkness is followed by tomorrow
   the shearing, carding, spinning, spooling
They're cripples of narration, time-sick, tense, tenseless,
   let's say, let's tell the one about the woman
They believe the fictional but not the serial as I do
   belatedly beautiful, or the man damaged in
nap, afraid to wake, awake with the whole utility
   the can't, the don't, the yes but, the not
of the world and the burden of flayed faces
   who would want a past, that story
that makes a woman a fetus and a man a haze
   Spring rain. Wish I could be reborn
as small a man as a violet.

TERESA STARR

At the Headstone for Hart Crane

"Thy absence overflows the rose"
—Hart Crane

Because from the humid bed of August
the afternoon held its blue arm out to me,
I stood on a hill in Garretsville, Ohio
at the headstone for Hart Crane—
one shared by Clarence Crane, his father.
As clouds removed all color from the sky,
their shadows clarified the grayness in his stone:
Harold Hart Crane, 1899–1932, Lost at Sea,
its granite pitted in spots by storms.
Even the weeds around it seemed to have died
looking into its rough surface.
But where was the lush sun he loved,
bright as a marigold, and as pungent?
Cicadas had not yet pierced the air
with their sharp percussion, nor was any wind
lost in the shallow grass, tipped with brown,
or in the dry limbs of the juniper and spruces—
only a cardinal dipping into stillness,
stretched between the seasons.
For a long time, among the vine-collared trees
I stood, wanting the breeze to raise itself
and cool me. Two ravens wavered
between the chiseled currents of their flight, longing
to fill the space where last night's stars had fallen.
And then, brushing a twig and some crumbling leaves away,
I wondered why I'd brought this rose
for a grave without a body.

Elsewhere

Not here, where the birds
pound their beaks on the rail
and the blue jay feeds before the sparrow
and a dried pot of mums holds a frozen pink flower,
no, not here but elsewhere.
Not here, where the grass
no longer wonders
or cares if the wind beheads a sunflower
under the terror of these clear skies,
no, not here but elsewhere.

There, that other place we stray
where you love me more
than I love you
and I bow like the fir to this sickness I feel,
no, not there but elsewhere.
There, birds bash
their beaks on the rail
and the squirrel eats corn before the jay
who eats thistle before the sparrow,
but not in seasonless elsewhere.

Elsewhere, beyond
the borders of these noons,
behind the sparrow waiting at the feeder,
no birds or flowers, no squirrels or trees,
elsewhere we live in peace.
But here, the sun
gives up its dream
and shells surround an empty feeder.
Elsewhere, the sun never bows;
here, everything's covered in shadow.

MARC J. STRAUS

Sigh

I sighed this morning, a slow deep inspiration
that dragged the air into the recesses of my lungs,
portions I imagine had been forgotten
in the last few months. And then for a second
or two I felt the life pass out of me.
As if it were a prelude, a taste for the sake
of recognition, to diminish my anger.
As if it were a gift to make me more accepting,
so that when the angel lifts my hand
onto her atom-less sleeve I will have no animosity.
She is so like my physician. He has no tolerance
for remonstration, his head is so cluttered
with obligatory data. I might articulate my pain
but he is filled with dying and I'm obliged
to keep the sigh inside.

Pinguid

I came across this word unexpectedly.
It means fatty, greasy, unctuous—I can't say exactly
since I've not seen it before. That's the beauty
of language—such surprise and variation, each synonym
a slightly different meaning. I think of unctuous
as a wormy, mealy-mouthed flatterer; greasy, a male:
disingenuous, pomaded, cigarette dangling
from mouth. It's in these nuances that we position
ourselves. Today, a patient asked me to explain
highly mitotic. It was on her biopsy report. She said
the dictionary described it as cell division.
It doesn't mean exactly that, I said. Then what?
she asked. Words sometimes take on special meanings,
I explained. It's dependent on the context, the background
of the person using it. So what does it mean, then?
she pressed again. I thought for a second about how
I might answer, craft an accurate explanation,
tinge the meaning with ambiguity, how it might slip
along the surface, viscous and opaque, pinguid and smooth.

TERESE SVOBODA

To My Brother, On the Occasion of His Second Breakdown

In such darkness you're not listening:
bees, corn, and tumescence
take up space, silence the landscape.
The hour of your seeming quiet
soon passes, plowed under.

If I trouble your sinking so much
you see the bottom
and the matching silences of moth,
money, and the worm, am I a prophet,
or is it foretold,
the deft seed whirling from a height?

The fury and majesty of a mind's death
I can't watch enough of
to keep you from teasing it closer,
your innocence springing clear too far
to be of any use but in blasphemy,
what you fall into

in such silence. You are deep inside, I believe,
beaded with tears.
If dollars wave in the fields, blood floods them,
and the dark grains pollinate and must be cut.
Let the winnowed make a drink like Lethe's.
If you survive, Death is the Other.

Children of Our Era

—translated from the Polish by Joanna Trzeciak

We are children of our era,
the era is political.

All affairs, day and night,
yours, ours, theirs,
are political affairs.

Like it or not,
your genes have a political past,
your skin a political cast,
your eyes a political aspect.

What you say, has a resonance,
what you are silent about, is telling.
Either way, it's political.

Even when you head for the hills
you're taking political steps
on political ground.

Apolitical poems are also political,
and above, a moon shines,
an object already non-lunar.
To be or not to be, that is the question.
What is the question? Darling, here's a suggestion:
a political question.

You don't even have to be a human being
to gain a political significance.
Crude oil will do,
or concentrated feed, or any raw material.

Or even a conference table whose shape
was disputed for months:
should we negotiate life and death
at a round table or a square one?

Meanwhile people were dying,
animals perishing,
houses burning,
and fields growing wild,
just as in eras most remote
and less political.

Reality Demands

Reality demands
we also state the following:
life goes on.
It does so at Cannae and Borodino,
at Kosovo Polje and in Guernica.

There is a gas station
in a small plaza in Jericho,
and freshly painted
benches near Bila Hora.
Letters travel
between Pearl Harbor and Hastings,
a furniture truck passes
before the eyes of the lion of Cheronea,
and only an atmospheric front advances
towards the blossoming orchards near Verdun.

There is so much of Everything,
that Nothing is quite well-concealed.
Music flows
from yachts at Actium
and couples onboard dance in the sunlight.

So much keeps happening,
that it must be happening everywhere.
Where stone is heaped on stone,
there is an ice cream truck
besieged by children.
Where Hiroshima had been,
Hiroshima is again
manufacturing products
for everyday use.

Not without its charms is this terrible world,
not without its mornings
worth our waking.

In the fields of Maciejowice
the grass is green
and on the grass is—you know how grass is—
transparent dew.

Maybe there are no fields other than battlefields,
those still remembered,
and those long forgotten,
birch woods and cedar woods,
snows and sands, iridescent swamps,
and ravines of dark defeat
where today, in sudden need,
you squat behind a bush.

What moral flows from this? Probably none.
But what really flows is quickly-drying blood,
and as always, some rivers and clouds.

On the tragic mountain passes
the wind blows hats off heads
and we cannot help—
but laugh.

DANIEL TOBIN

Eye-Full Tower

Where a love-dock jutted into the Narrows
I took turns with friends at a crack of light
someone scraped into the one black window
of The Eye-Full Tower, and saw through the tight
crush of men a woman dancing naked,
her sequined bridle glittering down her breasts
drenched in luminous sweat and smoke-haze.
From one she snatched a lit cigarette
and, her face blasé as a goddess's,
blew smoke rings at the howling crowd.
I rose then to my own loneliness,
eyeing with those men what floated on a cloud:
each ring a zero dispersing in space,
the hope born of the heart's raw promise.

The Crying Room

The church had a crying room—
up at the opposite side of the altar.
Good for the baby.
It was glass on all sides like a tank.
A microphone brought in the priest's voice.
From the crying room we could see
how things happened backstage:
someone coming to the priest
with a bell and a napkin.
We weren't soundproof.
Every time the baby cried
a pewful turned to us.
But then, after a point,
the parishioners were almost used to
the intermittent little shrieks,
the baby wanting down,
wanting up.
This was in a town
with the sea just a block away
and remarkable sea winds,
winds to lift, to accost, to warn.
I was holding the crying baby
behind the glass doors.
I could look out at the parishioners
who had gone to the trouble
to make a place for the smallest
throats among them,
even though they were used
to being pushed by invisible forces.
They were right to put distractions

ahead of them in glass
as if to preserve and in
preserving to distort,
and yet not fail to see
exactly who made trouble for them.

CHARLES HARPER WEBB

Biblical Also-rans

Hanoch, Pallu, Hezron, Carmi,
Jemuel, Ohad, Zohar, Shuni:
one *Genesis* mention's all you got.

Ziphion, Muppim, Arodi: lost
in a list even the most devout skip over
like small towns on the road to L.A.

How tall were you, Shillim?
What was your favorite color, Ard?
Did you love your wife, Iob?

Not even her name survives.
Adam, Eve, Abel, Cain—
these are the stars crowds surge to see.

Each hour thousands of Josephs,
Jacobs, Benjamins are born.
How many Oholibamahs? How many

Mizzahs draw first breath today?
Gatam, Kenaz, Reuel? Sidemen
in the band. Waiters who bring

the Perignon and disappear.
Yet they loved dawn's garnet light
as much as Moses did. They drank

wine with as much delight.
I thought my life would line me up
with Samuel, Isaac, Joshua.

Instead I stand with Basemath, Hoglah,
Ammihud. Theirs are the names
I honor; theirs, the deaths I feel,

their children's tears loud as any
on the corpse of Abraham, their smiles
as missed, the earth as desolate

without them: Pebbles on a hill.
Crumbs carried off by ants.
Jeush. Dishan. Nahath. Shammah.

The Night Sky

Rodney shifted the heavy wooden console a few inches each night, hoping the hotel manager wouldn't notice the newly revealed depression in the commercial-grade carpet. By the end of the week he could comfortably stand at the far left-hand side of the desk—actually a long laminated counter—and see the entire picture without distortion. He stood there now, watching the final minutes of a National Basketball Association playoff game.

Having decided to drop out of college at least until the fall, he had taken the night clerk job with the expectation that he would witness clandestine, even exotic behavior. At first he imagined every lone late-night arrival to be a criminal one step ahead of the law, every couple to be engaging in strenuous, costumed intercourse. Occasionally a couple checked in whom he was sure were having an affair—local address, no bags, more excited than weary—but the unresolved mysteries of the hotel's guests soon gave way to the tedium of long, quiet hours. On a typical night he watched television until 12:30, then read a paperback until the sun beamed over the forested mountains beyond the opthamologist's office across the street.

Rodney had briefly considered the circumstances of a woman who had been staying on the second floor for nearly two weeks. She gave a local address, and one of the maids said her room was empty except for toiletries, a few clothes, and some papers, but there was no sign of a man—or, for that matter, another woman. Rodney saw her blue sedan enter the parking lot every night between midnight and one, always from the west, not from the highway exit. She appeared to be in her sixties, and her body was heavily rounded in a way that made it difficult for Rodney to stay interested in her secret, whatever it was. From the way she walked, it seemed she meant to climb the stairs, unlock the door, and collapse onto the bed.

* * *

Elizabeth did not collapse but sat on the edge of her bed, ignoring two upholstered chairs flanking the small circular table centered under a hanging lamp. In two weeks the bed had become hers, the way this room had become hers; while she hadn't moved the furniture, or taken down the undistinguished landscape print of the surrounding mountains, she felt as intensely identified by this room as by any room she had ever lived in. Her feet ached, but she did not remove her shoes. Instead she took off her glasses, setting them on the bed beside her, and cupped her face in her hands. Even this room, lit by a single fixture just outside the bathroom door, was too bright, and too large; only by pressing her hands over her forehead and eyes could she contain the world long enough to concentrate.

Though the effect was lessening, every night the opening of the hotel room door filled her with as much guilt as any illicit lover ever felt; she thought of Terry's affair, his childish, stereotypical midlife boyhood—though she wasn't convinced he had felt any guilt before she confronted him. They hadn't talked about when he had felt guilty. She knew enough, and Terry said enough. Only recently had she wondered if it would have been better to have talked it all through. In the years since, there had been a terrible vulnerability in their marriage, as if someone had let a poisonous snake loose in the house. For months you might forget about it, but one day, in the laundry room, you would catch a glimpse of mottled coils, or you would remember how, when you first moved here, there had been mice.

Given any opportunity, Terry would have discussed it. He believed in talking through every problem, every disagreement. Silence frustrated him. She knew how badly he wanted to explain it all, to tell her why he had gotten involved with his other woman, why he would never do it again—and, since telling her everything would relieve him, she would not let him talk. *Take it with you to your grave,* she remembered thinking. The memory made her shoulders knot, her forehead tighten. She had been embarrassed and ashamed, having fallen for his lies and excuses, refusing to believe that all the situational clichés of movies and television were coming true.

What she was doing now was no cliché. She had never heard of anyone doing it before. She imagined she knew how it felt to be a bad soldier: one who believed in the cause, but who nevertheless ran from battle. To add to her shame, her guilt and cowardice, Terry was quick to tell everyone that he had asked her to stay here. To lie was his idea.

They had known he was sick; two years ago the doctors hadn't been able to remove all of the cancer. Last month, when the dogwoods and tulips were blooming, they learned the inevitable had grown closer. "The situation," Dr. Foote told her, was worse. They could try the chemotherapy again, but at best it would slow the disease's progress. Rachel, who missed two classes to be there, had put one strong arm around her. Anticipating the worst, Elizabeth thought she might slump heavily, but when the news came she felt strangely buoyant; it was as if someone had just told her that the earth was inside out. As if she had stepped into a marsh and found herself peacefully suspended. Then discovered she was not quite able to walk, not able to swim.

Terry refused the chemotherapy. "I want to go out hairy," he said, trying to cheer them up. "I want apple pie and cheesecake— I want a goddamned prime rib." They talked of travel: Hawaii, Southern France, Australia, or back to Scotland, where they had spent the summer over a decade ago. "Antarctica," he proposed. "Just to see a circle of those male emperor penguins holding eggs on their feet." In a serious moment, he admitted he didn't want to be far from home.

"I could take incompletes," Rachel told him. She was in her junior year at the state university in the city, majoring in education and theater, playing varsity volleyball.

"No need," Terry said. "But if you'd like to come around for dinner more often, I think we could find an extra plate."

So that's how he's going to be, Elizabeth thought. Stoic. He had succumbed to weakness the first time; the radiation and chemo had made him miserable. He was embarrassed about having been such a bad—scared, needy—patient. Bob Martin, one of her colleagues in the math department, had given her a quotation about "the kingdom of the sick." It ended: "Sooner or later each of us is obliged, at least for a spell, to identify ourselves as citizens of that other place."

Those first nights after Dr. Foote quietly estimated two months, six at the outside, they stayed awake together to consider and reject traveling plans, meals he would enjoy while he was still hungry, movies he wanted to see, friends and family who should visit. Then Terry began to return to routine. He watched the day's sports summary at eleven, attended to his teeth—first flossing, then brushing, then massaging his gums with a special small-bristled brush the dentist had prescribed—then read around in a magazine or a book until it fell on his chest. She would prod him awake; he would set the book on the floor, turn off his bedside light, and roll onto his side. He offered a single kiss, scented with the faint remains of aftershave or, more often now that the weather was warmer, sour perspiration.

Elizabeth could not sleep. After dinner she busied herself with the dishes and cleaning, then they would take a walk. She taught trigonometry and geometry at one of the county high schools, and there was grading to do. Her department was one of four statewide participating in a three-year study of the effective teaching of national standards, so two or three times a week she was obliged to log on to a computer bulletin board and correspond with other participants in the study. When she couldn't concentrate on that, she went back down to the living room. Some nights they played backgammon; others they watched television, or a movie. When the sports came on, she got ready for bed, and when Terry came to the bedroom, she pretended to read, or to sleep.

A woman at the hospital had given her information on counseling for family members of patients with terminal illnesses. This is what they would talk about, she thought: gathering important papers, evaluating your financial situation, learning how to take on new responsibilities. Elizabeth paid their bills and balanced the checkbook, and they made decisions about investments together. When Rachel was born, Terry insisted on buying what Elizabeth argued was far too much life insurance; when the policy arrived, he pretended to read from the envelope: "You May Have Won a Million Dollars." She wasn't scared about money. She worried about being alone, and her worry surfaced in absurd details. He did things to the cars and lawn mower, things she had never bothered to ask about, and now it was unthinkable. In the yard, he pruned what needed to be pruned, thinned what needed to be thinned, watered and fertilized with results such that friends were always asking him for advice. He knew how the Christmas decorations were most efficiently packed in the storage space under the stairwell, he knew what colors of stain they had used on the house and trim three years ago, he knew how to program the VCR. All things she could learn. Things she dreaded having to learn.

What haunted her most was his physical presence: his thin, graying hair, his crooked teeth, the mole on his neck. Even the faded paisley pajama bottoms seemed a part of his body. He breathed through his mouth, but when his allergies were bad or he slept on his back, he snored loudly. He had an office worker's paunch, a flabby belly with an appendectomy scar. At one time or another she had had nearly every inch of his skin in her hands, on her tongue. The memory of those moments of intimacy most terrified her now as he lay beside her, large as life. There was something the boys at school were saying this spring, one of those momentarily popular all-occasion expressions: *Dead meat.* It could be used as a threat (*You touch me again and you're dead meat*) or an expression of resignation (*As soon as I saw the first problem, I was dead meat*). Like a bee at a picnic, the phrase buzzed behind and beside and around every thought. She hated the way Terry looked when he slept.

In the middle of honors geometry one morning, she paused, exhaustion passed over her, and she suddenly had no idea what she had been saying. Angela, one of the eager front-row girls, offered politely, "You were reminding us about the theorems."

What theorems? Elizabeth thought. What class is this? The moment, horrifying, stretched on. She thought she would have to leave the room.

"I'm very sorry," she said. "I seem to have lost my train of thought." Aaron, an exemplary student, suggested with great diplomacy that she had been referring to their work with triangles and cones in the fall to demonstrate the relationship of analytic geometry to demonstrative geometry. "Thank you," she said, genuinely grateful, and went on.

The next day she sat in her room during her free period meaning to write comments for the awards ceremony, only to be awakened by her fourth-period class.

That weekend she told Terry, "I have something horrible to

confess." He had been describing his plan to kill all the grass on the slope down to the driveway and create a new flower bed.

He looked up from his drawing.

"I don't think," she began, then realized what she had been about to say. *I don't think I can sleep beside you again.* "I haven't been sleeping well," she said.

"I know this is ungentlemanly," he told her, "but you've looked absolutely exhausted. I thought it was end-of-the-year overload."

He must have known, but he wouldn't say it.

She didn't want to cry. She was so tired. "Maybe it is," she allowed.

Terry suggested, "Why don't I sleep in Rachel's room tonight?"

"No." She spoke more loudly than she intended. She wanted to tell him, Stop being so generous.

She said, "You should have the big bed. I thought I'd try Rachel's, just until I catch up on my rest. I don't think I told you, but Friday I actually dozed off at my desk." She hadn't meant to tell him now.

"Have I been snoring?"

"No more than usual. I really think it's me."

Terry smiled at her across the dining room table. "I'll miss you. But whatever, sure. Get a good night's rest." He picked up a catalogue. "I'm thinking about making this border heaths and heathers, and they're not going to have a chance in the clay we've got here. With the retaining wall, we'll essentially create a huge planter. The summer heat might be too much for them, but they shouldn't get any afternoon sun if this works out..."

Rachel's room offered no comfort. The past accumulated on Elizabeth's chest the way she imagined it would if she were the one dying. Meeting Terry at school, that first awful date, the wonderful Indian dinner, seeing *Casablanca* in that horrible-smelling theater, his clumsy proposal, her mistake with the wedding invitations, first jobs, trying not to get pregnant, then trying to, losing the first two, finally getting all the way through with Rachel...why was she the one feeling this way, as if the door to the past was about to be shut tight, locked, sealed off? Why was she the one who felt she was suffocating, being drawn toward an unavoidable horror? Laying in her daughter's bed tortured her; she was the child, the one who couldn't understand, couldn't accept the simple fact. Was

Rachel thinking these things? Rachel had forgiven Terry the affair; did that somehow make it easier for her to accept this? Elizabeth pictured the three of them as an isosceles triangle, then realized the sides should be uneven. Were Rachel and Terry closer to each other than she was to either of them, or was Terry the distant point? She pictured triangles turning like images on her computer monitor, turning in space but also distorted by time. She imagined three triangles, one to represent the way each of them saw their family—or was it that she saw it three different ways? She saw the triangles overlaid, imagined her parents, Terry's, the other woman, Rachel's roommate and boyfriend, the two children she had lost—all points on a star, then distinct stars, some bright, some faint. She tried to count them all.

She awoke without having slept. Her head ached, her body was sore. Sunlight pierced the curtains, glaring over Rachel's high school memorabilia. She smelled coffee, which Terry no longer drank, so must have brewed for her. Lying in her daughter's bed, she thought, I want someone to take care of me. Repulsed by her selfishness, she rose to shower.

"I've been feeling guilty," Terry announced. Sitting on the edge of the jetted tub, he handed her a warm cup when she finished drying off. With the word *guilty*, the snake dropped into view. He continued, "I'm guessing these new beds, hardscaping, plants, mulch, the whole nine yards, will run two thousand dollars."

In this room, the trees in front of the house filtered the sunlight. Despite the coffee, Elizabeth felt a chill. "Beds plural?"

"Still that one area, but I'm thinking it needs some steps." Squinting, she saw he was cleaning her glasses for her. He held them out. "I could be talked out of that. Anyway, my argument is that it's still a lot cheaper than the chemo. Or a trip to the Loire Valley. However you want to think of it."

Vision corrected, she glanced into the mirror expecting to see bags under her eyes. Craving sleep, she drank coffee.

"You know," she told Terry, "it's fine with me. Whatever you want to do." She headed toward the closet, leaving him on the side of the tub.

"If you're serious," he called after her, "I'm going to call some people, get some estimates on the labor."

The walk-in closet allowed just one person to stand between

the lines of clothes, shoes regimented below, sweaters stacked on the head-high shelf. She put her hand out, comforted by the cloth all around. She should put a pillow down in here.

When she came out he was sitting on the end of the bed. Their room, like Rachel's, got the morning sun. The light angled across Terry so that his outline, particularly his head, seemed to glow. He was already gone.

"Sleep any better?"

"It helped." She pulled on a sweatshirt, fighting off the chill.

"You," he said, "are a rotten liar."

But you've always been such a good one, she thought.

When that night was no different—she last checked Rachel's clock, a wall-mounted Elvis Presley whose hips shifted with each tick and tock, at 3:45, but doubted she drifted off before 4:30— she nearly wept from exhaustion. Now the phrase that repeated itself was a throbbing *I'm so tired, so tired.* It reminded her of a Beatles song, but she couldn't recall the rest of the lyric. The thought of going to school the next morning was nearly unbearable.

"Maybe I should try a hotel," she suggested at lunch, trying to sound facetious. She made chicken salad sandwiches. She was starving; she had no appetite. Her body didn't know what it wanted. Sleep.

"You don't feel sick?" Terry asked. "You aren't being a martyr?"

"I feel all right," she said, carrying the sandwiches through the sliding glass door to the patio. "I'm just—"

She couldn't stop; tears pooled in her eyes. "I'm so *tired!*" She sat heavily on one of the comfortless wrought-iron chairs, one of Terry's choices. They looked like something in one of the fine homes magazines, but she had never liked them. Now she thought, I shouldn't have to sit in this hard chair.

That night, after the awkwardness of checking in, certain even the desk clerk knew what she was avoiding, she turned on the television for distraction, lay down, and woke with the alarm she almost hadn't bothered to set.

Rachel moved back home. There was only a week left in the semester, followed by final exams. She was glad for the excuse to have more time near her father, but worried about her mother.

Even when she was rested, Elizabeth carried a hint of desperation around the edges, a woman on the verge. She devoted herself to her work at school, staying late as extracurricular projects met their end, had the members of the math team over for their annual dinner. They finished third in the state this year.

Rachel had a lifeguarding job for the summer, her ongoing gig at the country club pool. The pay was good—lifeguards were in high demand these days, she had turned down a dozen jobs—but she wondered if she shouldn't be doing something more career-oriented by now. She thought about applying for a position as summer school tutor, but the idea of staying indoors all day was too dreary. Maybe next year.

She immediately understood her father's plans for the hillside.

"We can put the heathers in this fall," he said, handing her the plant list, "but most of the perennials should wait until spring. Not the daylilies, or the peonies. But the butterfly weed and echinacea and liatris. I'd rather let the beds settle over the winter." He had bought a planning kit which included a large green cardboard grid, the surface treated so it could be written on with a wax pencil. The kit also included dozens of stickers, green branches on smaller and larger circles meant to represent plants. Terry, who had been a design engineer for a tool company, had carefully measured off the length and curve of the hillside and transcribed it here, to scale.

"What are these big ones?" she asked, pointing to the largest circles, each penciled with a number 7.

"Dogwoods. I was thinking two white, one pink." He had gone back and forth over the steps. In the current plan, they didn't appear.

"I'll have to label all these," he admitted. "I've got names and numbers there on the list, but it's a mess. I'll mark which come from which catalogues. Most of them you should be able to get around here."

He wasn't deceiving himself; he knew he wouldn't see the work finished. That's why Rachel decided she would spend the summer helping. It was impossible for her to think of preparing the ground without picturing his grave being dug, but she liked the idea that, instead of a tombstone, he would have this: not just the yard, with the footbridge he had built over the creek that rarely ran, and the hemlocks and sugar maples he had planted when he and her mother built the house, but this last creation, his attempt not at immortality—plants had their cycles, in a dozen or fifteen years the heathers would be spent—but at life transferred.

As Terry had feared, the best landscapers were booked at least until August. Rachel suggested that he hire strong arms and backs; as long as he supervised, they didn't need experienced help. Reynolds, a biology major she had been seeing, and his friend Christian had intended to spend the summer traveling, but those plans were stalled by lack of funds. Soon she found herself impatient sitting high in the lifeguard chair, oiling herself hourly to ward off skin cancer, watching the swimmers all around her: children hoping she wouldn't see them running on wet cement, some pretending to drown, some straining to dunk each other, one or two people floating, and a few calmly treading water, making slow progress against the length of the pool. At six o'clock she could put shorts on over her suit; at home she would find Terry measuring, adjusting the strings tied to pegs across the slope, as Reynolds and Christian dug.

"The bottom course of timbers is the slowest," he reassured them as the young men sat, shirtless, drinking beer from bottles. "Once they go in level, we'll get the rest up in two days, three at the most."

"I need calluses," Reynolds told Rachel, showing her his hands. Blisters had formed and torn open.

"Doesn't that hurt?"

He held up the bottle. "I take one of these every hour."

They were all inspired by Terry's refusal to complain. Occasionally he would stop in the middle of leveling a spot, walk a few steps away, and slowly sit. Sometimes he looked down; sometimes he rested his forehead on his knees, so that the brim of his baseball cap tilted high, revealing arches of hair. Reynolds and Christian responded by continuing their work; when Rachel was there, if her father looked particularly drawn, she would walk over and sit behind him, put one leg on either side, and lean her chest against his back. *Not today,* she thought. *Not yet.*

On one of these occasions he must have read her mind. So softly she could barely hear, he said, "I'm not going anywhere."

She couldn't tell whether he was optimistic or resigned.

A moment later he raised his head. She stared at the back of his neck, the soft creases of flesh, the mole on his left side. He said, "I worry about your mother."

She nodded. Then said, "She's scared."

He didn't respond. At times like this, she believed her father had secrets. Other times she knew there was nothing as simple as a mystery, no dramatic revelation. She wanted him to tell her about his parents; his life, beginning with his earliest memory; everything he had aspired to, every possibility he had decided against. But that was too much; and there was no single thing she most wanted to know. She wanted what only he could tell her, the way he would tell it. She wanted him.

With his left hand, Terry covered her knee. Squeezed.

Elizabeth came home for dinner. From then until bedtime their schedule was the same as ever, except that she stayed dressed while he read, and when he finally dozed off, instead of prodding him, she sneaked away. That's how it felt.

"You don't have to wait," he told her one night. "Unless, of course, you *want* to see the baseball highlights."

Elizabeth said, "I want to be with you."

Come watch the dying man, Terry thought. His anger rose closer to the surface each day.

He said, "Maybe we should do something." True, his time felt precious. Even so, he liked baseball, had always liked baseball, the game without a clock, and reading the box scores didn't replace seeing the day's home runs and final outs.

"Let's sit outside," Elizabeth suggested. "It's beautiful out tonight."

He watched the Orioles' centerfielder disappoint Boston fans with a ninth-inning homer, then tapped the remote control. "Sure."

On the patio, Rachel had been about to turn on the floodlights when Elizabeth said, "Let's just look for a minute."

He looked at the worksite, where the first layers of timbers were finally straight and level. The boys were strong, but they didn't appreciate what dirt could do to a wall. If the rebar didn't extend deep into the ground, if the timbers weren't stepped slightly back, in a few years the pressure of the earth would push them forward. The boys had been impatient, but now the hardest work was finished.

Eyes adjusting to the dark, he looked at the curve of hemlocks around back, the rhododendron silhouette that concealed a mahogany bench. He had intended to sink a pond there, with lilies and cattails and fish. He looked up at the maples and oaks, the tulip poplar with its tall, crooked trunk. He had meant to cut that down. Poplars were fast-growing, weak, and this one was close to the house. But there had been a poplar in their yard when he was young, and so this one lived, protected by sentiment. Was that foolish? Was he being foolish again, dragging them all through this construction? How should he be spending this time? He intended to make lists for Elizabeth, reminding her what to do, explaining things he had done. Was this an act of ego? The world would go on without him.

A bat flitted by.

Elizabeth said, "There's the Big Dipper."

"Where?" Rachel asked.

Elizabeth pointed out the arced handle, the angled bowl. "Isn't there a way, once you've got the Dipper, to see the North Star?"

That jogged a memory. "Follow the handle?" he asked.

"Just two of them," Elizabeth corrected. The longer they looked, the more stars appeared, as if their very looking created dots of light. "But which ones?"

"Look north," Rachel said logically. But now there were countless stars visible, with no telling which was the benchmark of their sky.

They all slouched in their chairs, faces tilted back as if to receive the light of the sun, or a dentist's drill. Rachel asked, "How many constellations do you know?"

The sparks above them revealed no design. Terry turned his head, wondered if that reddish one was Mars.

"Well, the Little Dipper," Elizabeth said. "And Orion."

How many nights had he done this? How many times had he looked up without ever bothering to locate himself among the stars? He remembered the childhood diversion of sitting on a sofa or bed, tilting his head backwards over the edge, and imagining the world where he would walk on ceilings, step up to pass through doors, duck under tall furniture. He remembered the sound of his mother's old canister vacuum drawing closer, its yellow light shining as she threatened to suck up his hair. What could he have been? Five?

"Here's what we'll do," he told his wife and daughter. "We'll get a good book, and maybe a star chart, and we'll learn the constellations together."

The next evening, after Reynolds and Christian had finished their beers and the coals had grayed in the grill, Rachel arrived.

"Hey," she said from the bottom of the hill. "It's a wall."

The retaining wall, now two feet high and forty feet long, with angled ends anchoring it in the hill, was nearly finished. After laying the top row they would give all of the timbers a final coat of stain with the sprayer. He had bought locust, which wouldn't rot, but he wanted the extra protection.

"Do lifeguards eat tuna?" he called as she brought two plastic bags from the car.

"We aren't picky," she told him. "Around four o'clock I nearly ate a toddler."

He watched the boys watch his daughter follow the brick walkway to the patio. In cutoff shorts over her close-fitting swimsuit, strong legs leading to worn sneakers, her long brown hair pulled through the gap in back of a baseball cap, she looked like an advertisement for summer.

"I went hog wild." Rachel set her bags on the iron garden table and began pulling things out. "I found two computer programs on the solar system, a neat-looking old book by the guy who wrote *Curious George*—remember, about the monkey?—a glow-in-the-dark star chart, and another little book that tells you the names of everything."

Terry looked and read the title, *A Guide to the Night Sky*. "Everything but a telescope."

Reynolds said, "You know that camera shop in the mall? They sell binoculars and lenses. I bet they'd have them."

Rachel put her purchases back into their bags. "More beers?" she asked the boys.

Terry felt it coming, and when Rachel came back with three bottles, having already twisted off the caps, and sat casually, knees spread the way girls' never spread their knees when he was young, the wave fell onto him. She would get married, have a house, children, job, a life so long that this day, if she could remember it, would be a faint moment in the distant past. He would be memories to her; to her children he would be photographs and occasional boring stories. Standing on the patio beside the stone wall he had built, surrounded by greenery he had planted, outside of the house he designed, he felt like a ghost. He would be forgotten the way fire forgets coal.

"I'll be back," he told them, both to remind them that he was there and to reassure himself. Sitting on the living room sofa, he gathered his strength, as he had to more and more often. He would not think this way. He would not yield to self-pity. As much as he wanted to talk about it all—the fatigue, the irrational hope, the betrayal of being eaten from the inside, the crush of regret—he would not. He would not ask Elizabeth for forgiveness, because now she had no choice but to forgive him. He would not pray, because his entire adult life he had been a nonbeliever. He would not ask why no one asked him what he was thinking. He had been genuinely relieved when Elizabeth suggested spending a night in Rachel's room; it was at night, after he worked to read himself to sleep, that his fate confronted him. Now he could curl on his side without worrying that Elizabeth would stop pretending to be asleep. She pretended during the day as well: she never mentioned that he stood less and less, moving from one seat to another, that he no longer reached for or held anything over his head, that his stride was shorter. He wanted to make love with her, but he refused to ask, because she could not refuse. *And I heard a voice from heaven saying unto me, seal up those things which the seven thunders uttered, and write them not.* This was his gift to them.

Terry had been right: Mars.

"Without a telescope," Rachel reported, "we should eventually be able to see all of the planets except Neptune, Uranus, and Pluto."

The three of them sat on the patio in the dark. Elizabeth had brought one of the captain's chairs from the den.

"As for constellations," Rachel continued, glancing at the dimly glowing star chart in her hand, "there's the Big Dipper. The pointers, on the outside, go up to Polaris. The handle and top of the Dipper are half of the spine of Ursa Major—the end of the handle would be the tail. And Polaris is the end of the handle of the Little Dipper."

"Slow down," Elizabeth said.

"Little Richard," Terry told her. "Right next to the Big Bopper."

"You see Polaris?" Rachel asked.

Elizabeth said, "I think so. That one?"

Rachel pointed. "That one."

"What's that other bright star, on the left?"

Terry told her, "That's the sun."

"Kochap," Rachel corrected. "The end of the Dipper. Now you should be able to connect them with those one, two . . ."

"I see it," Terry said. "Three stars in between, and another brightish on the far corner, for the bottom of the basket."

"Dipper," Elizabeth corrected. "Going that way." She drew a line in the air with her finger. "As if someone is pouring something out of the Little Dipper into the big one."

After installing the computer programs, Elizabeth had poked around in them. You could visit the planets, click so they slid into cutaway views, click them into orbit, animate Saturn's rings, learn the years Neptune was more distant from the sun than Pluto, and, disturbingly, see how the sun would eventually devour Venus, Mercury, and perhaps even Earth five billion or so years from now. With one click, the screen filled with the theoretical view from their longitude and latitude on this very day at this very moment. In a box in the lower right-hand corner, seconds ticked into minutes, minutes into hours. Time could be sped up, reversed, or stopped altogether. The sky could be viewed from Athens or Sydney, the globe could shift to put, say, Saturn front and center. With one click, stars were labeled; with another, the lines of the constellations were drawn; with yet another, elaborate drawings of mythological figures appeared. Three more clicks left the stars, dots of light on a monitor, alone.

"And that," Elizabeth said now, wishing the real sky were as bordered and orderly, "must be Cancer's southern claw." It was out before she thought.

"Where?" Terry asked.

She pointed it out.

Terry stared at the specks of light. Then said, "Well. No hard feelings."

The next night was overcast. H. A. Rey claimed, in his book, that coping with an obscured view was part of the challenge of learning the stars, but without the Big Dipper they were lost. Turning on one of the outside lights, Rachel read to them from *A Guide to the Night Sky.* "Listen to this: 'Many of the most recently-recognized constellations have no stories attached to them. These include Antila, the air pump; Fornax, the furnace; Horologium, the clock; and Norma, the carpenter's square.' Did you guys know about these?" She continued, " 'However, the vast majority of the constellations, particularly those most easily perceived by the unaided eye, carry with them tales which reveal little about the heavens, but much about those fascinated by wondrous objects afar.' "

Listening to her daughter's voice, Elizabeth found unexpected comfort. She was rested now. Each night the hotel bed welcomed her, its sheets pulled tight, the room vacuumed, a fresh bar of soap recently released from its wrapper resting by the sink. She was almost ready. At first she had only wanted to tell someone how angry she was. One night, searching for relevant discussions on the Internet, she came across a group of people talking about friends and relatives who had died horribly: drunken driving, Russian roulette, a brain hemorrhage. She had thought that on the computer, anonymous, she would be able to talk openly, but instead she simply lurked. It was the right word for how she felt. She recognized expressions of grief and loss familiar from bad books and television; they struck her as unoriginal, insufficient, and true. As her daughter's voice continued like a song she wanted to hear again, Elizabeth reached out in the direction of her husband.

Rachel remembered some of these stories. Reading this book's condensed versions of myths was similar, she thought, to looking at the stars; each chapter seemed unnaturally abrupt, but if you knew the context, there was sense to it all. Tomorrow she would buy a telescope, a strong one, so they could see everything. Early this morning, before the pool opened, she and Reynolds had made love in the clubhouse. "He's so brave," she had told him, thinking of her father even then. Every day that summer, the title of her job mocked her. What could she do? The wall was finished, the planting diagram complete. Terry explained that few people grew heathers this far south, but at their elevation, if the drainage was improved, and the bed had plenty of peat moss, they should thrive. The red and orange perennials would draw humming-birds, and butterflies. She asked questions, wanting to be able to finish what he had planned. What she couldn't ask him was, if her mother wouldn't sleep in the house now, what would she do once he was dead? Were they patronizing him, pretending they would keep this house, that they could keep what was his, without him to possess it?

Terry vaguely recognized a few of the stories of the constella-tions. What eluded him was the physics of the stars. Rachel had read them an article from the paper about an astronomer who claimed to have found another sun, a sun one million times brighter than Earth's, but so far away that it had never before been seen. How could that be? A million times brighter than the sun, and impossible to see.

He had always meant to read more of the classics. For half his life he had been aware of all the pursuits that would, in all likeli-hood, remain unpursued. And now, when he should feel free to take risks—go hang gliding, what's to lose?—he had dedicated his strength to self-control. He had thought at least he could stop the damned flossing every night, even brushing; but when he did, the next morning his teeth felt dirty. In some way he was grateful for the small irritation, the distraction.

Aaron, Elizabeth's best honors geometry student, was a text-book overachiever, preparing for tests by creating his own. In three years he would be accepted by both Harvard and Yale; in fif-teen he would be a successful cardiovascular surgeon. Tonight he sat up in bed, eating orange slices, rereading Sir Thomas More's *Utopia*, occasionally pausing to make notes. He had amused him-self by removing the orange's peel whole, then flattening it, which made him think *map*, and then *Gerardus Mercator*, the cartogra-pher whose collection of maps was the first to be called *Atlas*.

Above their heads, beyond the trees, constant in a boundless night, the stars stood fixed by shapes they yearned to know. Cetus. Cepheus. Andromeda.

ABOUT THOMAS LUX

A Profile by Stuart Dischell

Thomas Lux is always getting ready to leave for somewhere else: for the highway to his home in Waltham, Massachusetts, where he spends part of each week with his eleven-year-old daughter, Claudia; to his classes at Sarah Lawrence College, "each week a honk for Wallace Stevens" when passing through Hartford; to a writing residency at Warren Wilson or Cranbrook; to the airport for a newspaper assignment in San Diego or a poetry reading in Los Angeles, Ann Arbor, or Tucson. Lux is a tire manufacturer's dream and a frequent flier club's nightmare.

Of course, it wasn't always this way. Born in Northampton, Massachusetts, in 1946, he spent most of his childhood living on a small family dairy farm. His grandfather and uncle were farmers, and his father was the milkman. Sometimes Lux returns to that life in poems like "Barnfire," "The Milkman and His Son," and "Cows": "Trochee, trochee, trochee—that's how / I heard them, the cows..." Vividly it is remembered in "Triptych, Middle Panel Burning."

> It happened that my uncle liked to take my hand in his
> and with the other seize
> the electric cow fence: a little rural
> humor, don't get me wrong,
> no way child abuse...

And certainly not coincidentally in his recent poem "The Voice You Hear When You Read Silently":

> ...what you know by feeling,
> having felt. It is your voice
> saying, for example, the word barn...
> and a sensory constellation
> is lit: horse-gnawed stalls,
> hayloft, black heat tape wrapping
> a water pipe, a slippery
> spilled chirr of oats from a split sack,
> the bony, filthy haunches of cows...

Lux attended Emerson College in Boston. James Randall, his professor, recalls, "In the late 1960's when Lux came to us, the writing program was new. He looked vaguely like a hobo in dress and manner, but he stayed on. There was a freshness and openness about him, and he spread his enthusiasms to others. Before we knew it, we had a serious poetry group at our college." Upon graduation he was hired as Emerson's poet-in-residence. He then spent the fall of 1971 and the spring of 1972 at the Writers' Workshop at Iowa, but left before graduating to return to teach at Emerson. Appointments followed at Columbia College of Chicago, Oberlin, and then, in 1975, at Sarah Lawrence College, where he remains today. Additionally Lux has been on the graduate faculties of Iowa, Columbia, Boston University, Houston, Warren Wilson, Michigan, and Irvine.

James Randall published Lux's first chapbook, *The Land Sighted*, under the imprint of Pym-Randall, which was one of many small presses in the late sixties and seventies in a very active Boston publishing scene. Distinct among these small presses was Barn Dream Press, which Lux himself started with Joe Wilmott and Patrick Botacchi. Barn Dream published works by a group of young poets that included Bill Knott, Charles Wright, Marvin Bell, Paul Hannigan, and William Matthews.

Pym-Randall brought out *Memory's Handgrenade*, Lux's first full-length collection, in 1972. This was a productive decade in which he published three chapbooks and two more full-length collections, *The Glassblower's Breath* (Cleveland State, 1976) and *Sunday* (Houghton Mifflin, 1979). He has published four more collections of poems with Houghton Mifflin, *Half Promised Land* (1986), *The Drowned River* (1990), *Split Horizon* (1994), and, most recently, *New and Selected Poems: 1975–1995* (1997). In 1996, Adastra Press also issued *The Blind Swimmer: Early Selected Poems 1970–1975*. Additonally, Lux has published seven other chapbooks of poems.

Lux is a powerful advocate for the relevance of poetry in American culture. Those who wonder whether poetry can matter have probably never read him or attended one of his readings. A review of *New and Selected Poems* for the online bookseller Amazon.com comments, "His writing has escaped the confines of academia, bringing a ringing lyricism, raw humor, and a raging

Barnaby Hall

heart to the stuff of everyday life. More accessible than lofty his poems still retain a mysterious awe for language." Recently Lux gave eighteen readings in a little over two weeks at colleges, high schools, a prison, community centers, the lobby of the Château Marmont Hotel, and The World Stage in South Central Los Angeles. Lux's reading style is energized, dynamic, and entertaining. Elena Karina Byrne, a regional director for the Poetry Society of America, says: "Tom's readings come alive without pretension. With his 'heart like a tent peg pounded / toward the earth's core,' one hand raised in the air, he goes to work transforming the audience, using his own dependable wit and colloquial insight."

When asked why poetry suddenly has so many venues, Lux responds that he believes people want "what poetry, at its best, provides: something both complex and simple, something human and alive, something rarely overproduced but not lacking in its own kind of pyrotechnics. A lot of us feel overwhelmed in our lives by a popular culture dominated by technology, hugely overproduced movies and music. Poets have only one instrument. There are no backup singers for poets, no props, no synthesizers, no special effects. Just pure lucid words. Put in the proper order—which includes the order of their sounds—they can shake us to our bones."

PLOUGHSHARES

In both subject and syntactical inventiveness, Lux is public ene-
my number one against boredom. Just to list some titles of his
poems is instructive: "The Nazi at the Puppet Show," "What Mon-
tezuma Fed Cortes and His Men," "Commercial Leech Farming
Today," "Travelling Exhibition of Torture Instruments," "I Love
You Sweatheart," "The Oxymoron Sisters," "Walt Whitman's Brain
Dropped on Laboratory Floor," "Institute of Defectology," and
"Pecked to Death by Swans." At a time when many poets have
exclusively devoted themselves to explorations of the neurotic life,
Lux has expanded the breadth of his poems into the social fabric,
its weave and unraveling. His sense of outrage is non-polemical.
He does not offer bromides or remedies but reminds his readers of
humanity's horror, humor, and heart.

Michael Ryan, Lux's friend since their Iowa days, introduced
Lux at a poetry reading at the University of California at Irvine by
saying, "The generosity of spirit that makes him such a valued
teacher is also the ground beat of his poems. While he has been a
lyric poet since the beginning, singing of himself in a language
that has always been relentlessly inventive, he has in his maturity
developed the capacity to see clearly into other lives, including
the lives of historical figures, inanimate objects, words, and veg-
etables. His poems are like no one else's: readers of contemporary
poetry can recognize a Lux poem a mile away: their characteristic
wit, their refusal ever to be dull, their subjects and occasions
ranging from Edgar Allan Poe to endive, and sometimes, unfash-
ionably, their propounding of explicitly moral messages which
takes a tour-de-force virtuosity to get away with. The reason they
do and do brilliantly goes back to the writer's genuine generosity
of spirit: the creation of a humane, down-to-earth, and wise man
to speak the poems, who is not only in the poems, but has been
himself created in fact in no small part by twenty-five years of
writing them. Of all the poets I know, I know of none less suited
to do anything else—which is to say I know of no poet who is
able to give his work, and embody in his work, more of himself."

Lux's work has not gone unrecognized by other poets, editors,
reviewers, and foundations. He has received grants and awards
from dozens of organizations, including the Kingsley Tufts Award
for *Split Horizon,* the Jerome Shestack Poetry Prize from *The
American Poetry Review,* the Emily Clark Balch Award from *The*

Virginia Quarterly Review, the Alice Fay di Castagnola Award from the Poetry Society of America, a Guggenheim Foundation fellowship, and three fellowships from the National Endowment of the Arts.

Over the last few years, Lux has also written several feature articles on assignment for the weekly newspaper *The San Diego Reader.* One concerned dairy farming in the Pauma Valley, another was based on a visit to the Museum of Death in San Diego. In his most recent piece, "Poetry and the People," Lux provokes a nurse, a cop, two advocates for the homeless, and a rat-catching exterminator to each write a poem, urging them to simply find the voice within themselves, to listen to—as he defines in his own poem—"The Voice You Hear When You Read Silently":

> not the sound your friends know
> or the sound of a tape played back
> but your voice
> caught in the dark cathedral
> of your skull, your voice heard
> by an internal ear informed by internal abstracts
> and what you know by feeling...

Ryan's remarks on Lux's generosity remind me of an almost trivial incident that occurred some years ago. I had bought a new car, my first, and Tom and I took it for a spin and to get something for lunch. I noticed a highly coveted and unusually ample Cambridge parking space, nosed my car into the spot, and left lots of room to keep from getting bumped. An urban success. Walking to the restaurant, Lux looked back over his shoulder. He was aghast I had taken up two places. "What if some poor fucker like you is driving around looking for a place to park?" I got back in my car and made room.

Stuart Dischell is the author of two collections of poetry: Good Hope Road *(Viking), which was a National Poetry Series selection, and* Evenings & Avenues *(Penguin). He teaches in the M.F.A. program at the University of North Carolina, Greensboro.*

BOOKSHELF

Recommended Books · Winter 1998–99

THE END OF THE ALPHABET *Poems by Claudia Rankine. Grove,*
$20.00 cloth. Reviewed by Michael J. Carter.
In Claudia Rankine's new collection, *The End of the Alphabet*,
the always tenuous relationship between language and felt experi-
ence is stretched nearly to its limit: "The moment / of elucidation
snipped its tongue." Anguishing and fragmented, the voice in
these poems relies heavily on broken syntax, unreliable grammat-
ical structures—open parentheses and hyphens abound—because
inner and outer forms have collapsed. Here is a speaker operating
from severe dislocation, perhaps insanity, where the calculus
between internal and external realities is conflicted at best, disas-
sociated at worst. The book begins: "Difficult to pinpoint, / / fear
of self, uncoiled." Not a fresh idea, nor are these poems formally
striking, but what fuels this collection is the emotional current
and urgency of the writing.
   Idiosyncratic, *The End of the Alphabet* is a deeply embedded dia-
logue within the self. Without a coherent narrative, this dialogue
wrestles with the "inherent indeterminacy" of language and expe-
rience. "Assurance collapses naturally / as if each word were a
dozen rare birds / flown away. And gone / / elsewhere is their guar-
anteed landing." Unable to track within the common bounds of
meaning, Rankine's narrator, who refers to herself as Jane, floats
in a netherworld of displaced meaning. It's as if she were a post-
modern Persephone who has eaten the seeds of despair and must
carry them forth, back into the living world: "—wanting and the
body losing, all the time / losing, beforehand, inside." Yet this in-
sistent losing does lift in moments of recognition of the outside
world: "enveloped again by movement, before, finally, / the out-
side tap turns tentatively on—"
   The End of the Alphabet could have lapsed into myopia if it
didn't ascend occasionally out of the pressurized private dialogues
that mark much of the collection: "... Clearly, you know, / so say,
This earth untouched is ruptured enough to grieve." Beside the

lovely musicality of these lines lies a momentary transcendence into identification, a glimpse of the broken-hearted world. As Jane says, "Just as the lips open open the eyes." This is the crux of the book, "To locate the self salvaged." Yet to find one's self in the world depends in some part on the ability to give it form using language. The problem for the narrator is, "Our addiction to telling / is effort to shape what surfaces within the sane." And the speaker does not feel sane. "Vulgarized by breath, plundered, handed round, I ask you, *how / how to have lived this?*"

How indeed. Despair and loss of meaning in *The End of the Alphabet* are palpably realized by Rankine. This is a long look into the enervating dark of a postmodern soul fissured by loss. But this is not so much a depressing celebration of darkness as it is an attempt at healing (despite the overuse of that word in politics and self-help). As Rankine writes: "The day I am at peace I will have achieved / a kind of peace even I know suggests I am crazy. / But, as it will be how I survive, I will not feel so."

Michael J. Carter is a poet living in Boston. He is co-editor with Diann Blakely of Each Fugitive Moment, *a collection of essays on Lynda Hull.*

THE GIRL IN THE FLAMMABLE SKIRT *Stories by Aimee Bender. Doubleday, $21.95 cloth. Reviewed by Fred Leebron.*

All elements are on fire in Aimee Bender's startling and funny debut collection, *The Girl in the Flammable Skirt.* Set predominantly in San Francisco and parts unknown, these sixteen stories boldly and confidently explore the nature of failed relationships due to liplessness, ennui, and, in one case, a hole in the stomach.

"What You Left in the Ditch" is a touching tale about a veteran's wife coming to terms with his disfigured return from the war. In powerful, ironic, and declarative prose, the story begins: "Steven returned from the war without lips." Of course, he has plastic prostheses, but still, this is a bit too much for his wife, Mary. In search of lips, she strays afield with a guy from a grocery store: "He stepped down to a lower plain so he was suddenly her height and she went into his face and kissed those lips, reminded herself. They were so soft. She kissed him for a moment, and then she had to move away; they were too soft, the softness was murdering her." In such spare prose, Bender's deft language connects the ironic world of surrealistic invention to the real world of pain and empathy, and indicates a writer who never takes the easy way out.

In "Quiet Please," a beautiful, grieving librarian takes a day at work to seduce every available man who approaches her desk, having each join her in the back room for "the sex that she wishes would split her open and murder her because she can't deal with a dead father; she's wished him dead so many times that now it's hard to tell the difference between fantasy and reality." It's no mistake that such an erotic run is confounded by the muscleman from a traveling circus: while such enactments of lust might be deadly, they are not as powerful as they seem.

One has the wonderful sensation reading this book that the stories, while playful and authoritative in content and style, insist on their own vulnerability. The narrator from "Fell This Girl," for instance, allows herself to yield to any seductor, even an old man "redder and sweaty, a sappy smile on his face." In the bar, she tells us, "I lay my arms across the top of the couch like I'm claiming the world, this is all mine, I'm so confident." Yet having escaped by story's end, she's absolutely exposed: "I will feel the wind fill up my dress and pass through me in tunnels until I am so numb with cold, I can't tell when we stop."

These are stories in which even the contemplation of a ceramic bowl will lead a character to considering the quicksand nature of sex and love, and in which a very skilled writer develops a voice of astonishing pace and wisdom. *The Girl in the Flammable Skirt* is an entertaining and powerful collection.

Fred Leebron is the author of the novel Out West *and co-editor of* Postmodern American Fiction: A Norton Anthology. *His new novel,* Six Figures, *is forthcoming from Knopf.*

FUEL *Poems by Naomi Shihab Nye. BOA Editions, $12.50 paper. Reviewed by Victoria Clausi.*

The poems in Naomi Shihab Nye's latest book, *Fuel,* comprise a world filled with intelligence, warmth, humor, and tenderness. It is a world wherein the ordinary becomes extraordinary and the lived moment links itself to history. It is a world in which the poet works with as much generosity in uniting the Arab and the Christian worlds as she does in bringing together a mother and her son for an evening at the ballet, or a classroom of pupils and their teacher, or a variety of lost pets and their owners, or a divorced friend and the "almost blooming" lying "dormant" within her.

Nye's best poems often act as conduits between opposing or distant forces. Yet these are not didactic poems that lead to forced epiphanic moments. Rather, the carefully crafted connections offer bridges on which readers might find their own stable footing, enabling them to peek over the railings at the lush scenery.

With clear images and striking metaphors, *Fuel* confirms Nye's belief in the value of the overlooked, the half-forgotten, "the little sucked-in breath of air / hiding everywhere." Like the late William Stafford, to whom Nye dedicates the second poem in this volume, "Bill's Beans," she cannot help loving small hidden wonders of the natural world. "Under the leaves, they're long and curling. / I pull a perfect question mark and two lean twins, / feeling the magnetic snap of stem, the ripened weight."

But Nye's Palestinian-American heritage, reflected in several of the strongest poems in *Fuel,* leads her to take up more worldly concerns as well. She never rails, though. Her poetics require a calmer language, her implicit claim being that a writer's impact increases when she becomes quieter, more contemplative. In "The Palestinians Have Given Up Parties," her distress about the devastated region where "once singing would rise / in sweet sirens over the hills" bears less anger than sorrow, less admonishment than prayer. In this poem, as in many others, Nye resolutely seeks to tell "the story behind the story." For Nye, the power of the lesson lies beyond headlines—the heartbreaking truth that "bombs break everyone's / sentences in half" and "soldiers come at night / to pluck the olive tree from its cool sleep." Nye insists her readers see more, that they feel, smell, and hear softer, smaller, quieter, and so, paradoxically, more powerful images: "No one hears the tiny sobbing / of the velvet in the drawer."

To know the poems of *Fuel* is to hear that "tiny sobbing"; it is to see "grasses in their lanky goldenness"; it is to smell the fundamentalism of "villagers carrying baskets of lemons"; it is to learn, again, the way we learned as children, how to "open, / when we are so full." One comes from this collection enlivened by the wisdom Nye finds in a range of subjects, spanning from the larger themes of war to the extraordinary "thanks" she gives "to the small toad that lives in cool mud at the base of the zinnias."

Victoria Clausi's poetry has appeared in The Squaw Review, Poetry Motel, *and* Visions International. *She teaches poetry and writing at O'More College in Franklin, Tennessee, and in Bennington College's July Program.*

CENTRAL SQUARE *A novel by George Packer. Graywolf, $24.95 cloth.* Reviewed by Don Lee.

There is a Cambridge, Massachusetts, with which few outsiders are familiar—the neighborhood that is the title of George Packer's second novel, Central Square, which squats between posh Harvard and MIT, blighting the main avenue with "its discount shops, foreign restaurants, secondhand music stores, social services, hawkers and idlers and unstable energy." As the neighborhood's diversity is being threatened by gentrification, as liberalism falls to yuppiefication, three residents struggle to maintain a sense of community and, in the process, to save themselves.

Paula Vorhees works as a therapist in a basement counseling center that is quaintly called the Problem Place. More and more, she feels spent and trivial, "like a hooker hired by the hour to coax vices, hand out Kleenex, make the client feel that she cared for no one less in the world.... Many of them told her it helped them to talk to her—that they had no one else in the world to talk to. Today this thought saddened her beyond words." She has problems of her own: an indifferent lover, an alcoholic mother, and the very real possibility that she'll lose her job. Funding for the center is dwindling, and her boss can't be bothered, preoccupied as he is with a nascent citizens group that bills itself as The Community—"a cross between a block watch, a nonviolent militia, and a twelve-step group." But when she meets Eric Barnes by chance one wintry evening, she staves off the bleakness for a little while, commencing an affair with him, trying hard to ignore the fact that he is married.

What Paula doesn't know is that Eric's wife, Jane, is very pregnant, a development that looms over him with a crushing magnitude. A thirty-seven-year-old writer, he is trying to eke out his fourth novel but is stymied by money problems, not to mention his wife's self-absorption. He asks his editor—a victim of mergers and acquisitions—for a bigger advance, and he is told that he will be lucky, with his paltry sales figures, to get his new book published at all. Eventually, he decides to discard his high-minded integrity and write an article for a slick magazine. "I've been an earnest little shithead, haven't I?" he says to Jane. He plans to focus the article on Joe, a young African who is part of the crew renovating his house, and who has mysteriously become an icon for The Community.

As it turns out, Joe is not really African, but merely an African-American drifter, originally from San Francisco. After being fired from his job at Kinko's, he had gone to Africa for a year to plant trees, yet fled back to the U.S. following a tribal slaughter. At the airport, and then again at a shelter called the Rainbow House, he is mistaken for an African national, and thereafter Joe happily allows rumors to flourish that he is a shaman, a healer, a magician, a shape-shifter. "He discovered that making things up was easier than telling the truth, which always felt like signing a confession. His new voice was deeper than the old one, and richer, and as he listened to its strange and wonderful sounds he began to think of a shy, elegant, skillful young African, full of promise."

Events culminate at a rally sponsored by The Community. Joe reveals his deception, nearly causing a riot, and Paula faces the futility of her affair with Eric, by now "aware of a weak strain in his character, a dutifulness that tended toward fatalism; a self-ful-filling conviction that life was bound to disappoint. He was not hard enough. He was not one of the winners." It is a brutal assessment, and *Central Square* is a searing, trenchant elegy of the passion that once fueled the ideals of socialism, love, spirituality, racial harmony, class, and art—all attempts to commune with a larger purpose. The novel's plot doesn't quite meet its potential, but Packer writes with intelligence and honesty, and *Central Square* stands not only as an evocation of a neighborhood, but also as an important survey of our culture.

*Books Recommended by
Our Advisory Editors*

George Garrett recommends *Dogfight and Other Stories*, a first collection by Michael Knight: "A strikingly original and various young writer." (Dutton)

Fanny Howe recommends *The Letters of Mina Harker*, a novel by Dodie Bellamy: "A contemporary epistolary novel that carries the ecstatic and personal extravagance of New York School poetry into a new realm. San Francisco but also novelistic observation. Sexually explicit but far from pornographic. See the difference." (Hard Press)

Jane Hirshfield recommends *Below Cold Mountain*, poems by Joseph Stroud: "One of the finest collections of poems I've read in years—intelligent, sensuous, moving, full of human insight." (Copper Canyon)

Dan Wakefield recommends *City of a Hundred Fires*, poems by Richard Blanco: "An exciting first book by a young Cuban American of great talent." (Pittsburgh)

EDITORS' CORNER

*New Books by
Our Advisory Editors*

Richard Ford, editor of *The Essential Tales of Chekhov*, stories translated by Constance Garnett: Ford selects twenty stories by the Russian master, including provocative lesser-known pieces by Chekhov in his youth, as well as widely anthologized classics. (Ecco)

George Garrett, *Bad Man Blues*, stories and essays: Subtitled *A Portable George Garrett*, this new book of stories, anecdotes, and personal essays shows Garrett at his playful and eloquent best. (SMU)

Tim O'Brien, *Tomcat in Love*, a novel: In his seventh novel, O'Brien makes a brave and hilarious turn with Thomas Chippering, a professor of linguistics, Vietnam vet, spurned husband, and unrivaled womanizer. (Broadway)

Chase Twichell, *The Snow Watcher*, poems: Twichell's fifth book presents an extraordinary sequence of poems that asks a single obsessive question: What is the self? This is a radical reenvisioning of what makes us human rather than animal. (Ontario)

Derek Walcott, *What the Twilight Says*, essays: In his first prose collection, Walcott brilliantly and lyrically discusses the works of Lowell, Brodsky, and other writers, and the state of West Indian literature and culture. (FSG)

Alan Williamson, *Res Publica*, poems: The title sequence of Williamson's new collection serves as a stunning elegy for Vietnam-era America and the war's aftermath of media saturation, multiculturalism, and violence. (Chicago)

POSTSCRIPTS

Miscellaneous Notes · Winter 1998–99

ZACHARIS AWARD *Ploughshares* and Emerson College are pleased to present David Gewanter with the eighth annual John C. Zacharis First Book Award for his collection of poems, *In the Belly,* which was published last year by the University of Chicago Press. The $1,500 award—which is funded by Emerson College and named after the college's former president—honors the best debut book published by a *Ploughshares* writer, alternating annually between poetry and fiction. This year's judge was the poet John Skoyles, who is a *Ploughshares* trustee.

David Gewanter was born in 1954 in New York City. The son of a pathologist and an art gallery entrepreneur, he was raised in New Jersey, New York, and principally in Ann Arbor, Michigan. For a brief time, Gewanter was a premed student at the University of Michigan, thinking he would follow in his father's footsteps and become a doctor, but his attention wandered, and he ended up majoring in Intellectual History. "I was an energetic but unfocused student, or overfocused on issues that weren't on the syllabus," he says. With only one term paper left to complete his undergraduate degree, he took "what I'll charitably call a hiatus" and parked himself in London for two years. There, he lived two doors down from John Keats's former house. After reading Keats's manuscripts, Gewanter was inspired for the first time to write his own poetry.

He returned to the U.S. and supported himself with all kinds of manual labor, from carpentry to jackhammering to driving a forklift. He also washed dishes for almost two years. "I tried to read Sophocles on my breaks," he recalls. "Not a good plan." Finally he finished his B.A. at Michigan, winning a Hopwood Award, then traveled to Barcelona and taught ESL for a year. He then went to the University of California at Berkeley, where he eventually earned a Ph.D. in English. Along the way, he took poetry workshops with Thom Gunn, Robert Pinsky, and Frank Bidart, and spent one semester at Harvard University, studying with Seamus Heaney. His poetry career went slowly, his first publications in *Occident* and *Poetry Flash*, then in *The Threepenny Review*, *Agni*, *New England Review*, *Tikkun*, *Ploughshares*, *Tri-Quarterly*, and the anthologies *The National Poetry Competition* and *New Voices*.

He moved to Cambridge, Massachusetts, and taught expository writing at Harvard, later directing two writing programs there. All the long while, he worked on *In the Belly*, which had begun as his master's degree thesis. "I kept adding new poems and throwing out the worst," Gewanter says. "The first and last poems of the book were among the last done. If the publisher hadn't accepted it, I'd still be tinkering."

In the Belly is structured into three parts that examine the body of a life: youth, romance, and family. At turns erudite and colloquial, always lyrical, the collection presents a voice with a maturity, technical mastery, and emotional weight that are extremely rare in first books. Poet Mark Doty writes: "These poems examine the body, the inescapable locus of desire and of loss, of persistence and of decay. Gewanter's careful ear and delicate eye are engaged in a sustained work of investigation: a struggle to find, in the difficult stuff of experience, what can be known, and said." John Skoyles comments about the book: "A stunning diction, a sinewy syntax, a true and convincing tone of voice: these are among the many qualities I admire in David Gewanter's *In the Belly*. From the first poem, 'Annals of the Wonder-Cabinet,' I felt drawn to read the words aloud, so inviting is their music and so compelling their subjects. I admire the necessity and finish of these wonderful poems."

Gewanter now lives in Washington, D.C., with his wife, the writer Joy Young, and their baby son. He is teaching poetry at Georgetown University and working on a new manuscript of poems, *The Sleep of Reason*, and a book of essays, *Identity Poetics*. He is also editing, with Frank Bidart, *The Collected Poems of Robert Lowell* for Farrar, Straus & Giroux.

The John C. Zacharis First Book Award was inaugurated in 1991. The past winners are: Carolyn Ferrell for *Don't Erase Me*;

Kevin Young for *Most Way Home;* Debra Spark for *Coconuts for the Saint;* Tony Hoagland for *Sweet Ruin;* Jessica Treadway for *Absent Without Leave;* Allison Joseph for *What Keeps Us Here;* and David Wong Louie for *The Pangs of Love.* The award is nominated by the advisory editors of *Ploughshares.* There is no formal application process; all writers who have been published in *Ploughshares* are eligible, and should simply direct two copies of their first book to our office.

VOLUNTEERS AND TRUSTEES We would like to recognize our interns and volunteers for their extraordinary efforts. In particular, our poetry and fiction readers, who are listed on the second page of the masthead, provide the yeoman service of screening the many unsolicited submissions we receive, and we would be paralyzed without them. Our thanks, too, to our trustees for their continuing support and assistance: Marillyn Zacharis, Jacqueline Liebergott, DeWitt Henry, Carol Houck Smith, Charles J. Beard, Frank Bidart, S. James Coppersmith, Elaine Markson, James Alan McPherson, and John Skoyles.

SUBSCRIBERS Please feel free to contact us by letter or e-mail with comments, address changes (the post office will not forward journals), or any problems with your subscription. Our e-mail address is: pshares@emerson.edu. Also, please note that on occasion we exchange mailing lists with other literary magazines and organizations. If you would like your name excluded from these exchanges, simply send us an e-mail message or a letter stating so.

CONTRIBUTORS' NOTES

CHRIS ADRIAN's fiction has appeared in *Story, The Paris Review, The New Yorker,* and *The Best American Stories 1998.* He lives in Virginia, where he is a medical student.

JON ANDERSON has just completed a new book manuscript, *So Long, Ernie Vanilla.* He teaches and lives in Tucson, and has published six previous books, including *In Sepia* and *The Milky Way.*

ANGELA BALL lives in Hattiesburg, Mississippi, where she teaches in the Center for Writers, University of Southern Mississippi. Her latest book of poetry is *The Museum of the Revolution: 58 Exhibits,* published by Carnegie Mellon University Press in January 1999.

SUSAN BERLIN's poems have been published in *Controlled Burn, Cincinnati Poetry Review, The Asheville Poetry Review,* and *Harvard Review,* among others. She is a recent nominee for *The Pushcart Prize XXIII.* She lives in Chatham, New Jersey.

LAURE-ANNE BOSSELAAR is the author of *The Hour Between Dog and Wolf* (BOA Editions, 1997). She is the editor of *Outsiders: Poems About Rebels, Exiles, and Renegades,* which is due out from Milkweed Editions in April 1999. She co-edited, with her husband Kurt Brown, *Night Out: Poems About Hotels, Motels, Restaurants, and Bars* (Milkweed, 1997).

KURT BROWN founded the Aspen Writers' Conference, and Writers' Conferences & Festivals (a national association of directors). He is the editor of *Drive, They Said: Poems About Americans and Their Cars* and *Verse & Universe: Poems About Science and Mathematics.* His first full-length collection of poetry, *Return of the Prodigals,* will be published by Four Way Books in 1999.

MICHAEL BYERS is the author of *The Coast of Good Intentions* (Houghton Mifflin, 1998), a book of stories. His work has appeared in various magazines and anthologies, including *The Best American Short Stories 1997.* A former Stegner Fellow, he now lives in Seattle.

ELENA KARINA BYRNE is Director of the Los Angeles chapter of the Poetry Society of America, and Poetry Consultant for the Getty's Research Institute. She is completing her first book of poems, *Sanctuary of Hunger,* and a book of essays, *Inseparable to Insignificance.* Her publications include *The American Poetry Review, Poetry, Denver Quarterly, The Colorado Review, The Virginia Quarterly,* and elsewhere.

JARI CHEVALIER's poems have appeared in *American Literary Review, 360 Degrees, Santa Barbara Review, Pivot,* and other literary magazines. She received her B.A. from Columbia University and her M.A. from City College of New York, where she was awarded an Academy of American Poets Prize. She teaches creative writing and lives in Ojai, California.

VINCENT CIOFFI is pursuing his M.F.A. in poetry at Sarah Lawrence College. Recent work has appeared or is forthcoming in *The Iconoclast* and *Parting Gifts*. He lives in southern Vermont with his wife, Laura, and their three sons, Mitchel, Jeremiah, and Michael.

SCOTT COFFEL's poetry has appeared in *The Antioch Review, Prairie Schooner, The American Scholar, The Wallace Stevens Journal, The Iowa Review, The Paris Review,* and *Salmagundi.* He lives in Iowa City with his wife and son.

BILLY COLLINS's most recent collection is *Picnic, Lightning* (Pittsburgh, 1998).

LUCY CORIN's fiction recently appeared in *The Southern Review.* Other stories, published under the name Lucy Hochman, have been in *The Iowa Review, The Mid-American Review, The North American Review,* and the anthologies *New Stories from the South 1997, Under 25: Fiction,* and *On the Edge: New Women's Fiction Anthology.* "Wizened" is included in her story manuscript, *Imaginary Wars in Bellford County.*

ROBERT DANBERG is a college administrator and teacher. His work has appeared in *Kerem* and *Literacy Harvest.* He lives with his wife, Mary Biggs, and his son, Rubin, in New York City.

CHARD DENIORD's poems and essays have appeared recently in *The Pushcart Prize XXII, The Gettysburg Review, Ploughshares, The Iowa Review, Agni, Harvard Review,* and *The Mississippi Review.* He is the author of *Asleep in the Fire* (Alabama, 1990). He teaches English, comparative religions, and philosophy at the Putney School in Vermont.

STEPHEN DOBYNS's most recent book of poems is *Common Carnage,* and his latest novel is *Saratoga Strongbox,* both from Viking. His book of essays on poetry, *Best Words, Best Order,* was published by St. Martin's Press in 1996. He lives in Watertown, Massachusetts.

SHERRY FAIRCHOK is a technical writer at IBM in White Plains, New York. She received her M.F.A. from Sarah Lawrence College in 1997 and was subsequently awarded a residency by the Constance Saltonstall Foundation of Ithaca, New York. Her poems have appeared in *Calyx, Passages North,* and *Cimarron Review.*

ROBERT FANNING received his B.A. from the University of Michigan and his M.F.A. from Sarah Lawrence College. Recently, he won the Foley Poetry Award. His poems have appeared in *The Hawaii Review* and *America.*

D. A. FEINFELD edited the literary magazine at the University of Rochester and currently studies poetry with Thomas Lux and Natalie Safir. His poems have appeared in *The Centennial Review, The Hollins Critic, Slant,* and *G.W. Review,* and his book, *What Do Numbers Dream Of?,* was recently published by University Editions.

TIMOTHY FERINE writes and lives in New York City. A graduate of Sarah Lawrence College, he is Poetry Editor of *Gimlet Eye*, an e-zine (www.gimleteye.com). He can be reached by e-mail at tferine@erols.com.

MICHAEL FITZGERALD is the author of ten books, most of them distributed by Kalimat Press of Los Angeles. His *Selected Poems 1984–1994* was published by George Ronald Publisher, Oxford, England. He also has eight recordings of music and poetry with Falling Mountain Music, an acoustic independent label. He studied at the Iowa Writers' Workshop.

RICHARD P. GABRIEL is a poet, essayist, and computer scientist. His most recent book is a collection of essays called *Patterns of Software: Tales from the Software Community*. His manuscript, *Leaf of My Puzzled Desire*, was a finalist for the National Poetry Series.

CHRISTINE GARREN's book of poems, *Afterworld*, was published by the University of Chicago Press in 1993 and was a finalist for *The Los Angeles Times* Book Award.

DOREEN GILDROY received her M.F.A. from Warren Wilson College. Her poems have appeared in *The American Poetry Review, The Antioch Review, The Colorado Review, The Marlboro Review, TriQuarterly, The Virginia Quarterly Review*, and *Volt*.

CINDY GOFF received her M.F.A. from George Mason University in 1993, and has since taught composition and literature courses at several colleges. Her poetry has appeared in many publications, including *Poetry East, The Quarterly, Exquisite Corpse, The Spoon River Poetry Review, The Indiana Review*, and the anthology *Last Call*. She currently lives in Warrenton, Virginia.

MARK HALPERIN has taught in Japan, Estonia, and Russia, and is a professor of English at Central Washington University. His poems and translations have appeared widely, and his most recent book of poems, *The Measure of Islands*, was published by Wesleyan. He and his wife, the painter Bobbie Halperin, live near the Yakima River, which he fishes avidly.

JAMES HAUG is the author of *The Stolen Car*, a collection of poems. The Center for Book Arts in New York has just published his chapbook, *Fox Luck*.

JOHN HAZARD teaches English at the Cranbrook Educational Community in Bloomfield Hills, Michigan. His poems have appeared in several magazines, including *Cincinnati Poetry Review, Poetry Northwest*, and *Passages North*.

ELIZABETH HOLMES is a freelance writer and editor in Ithaca, New York. Her poems have appeared in *Poetry, The Gettysburg Review, Michigan Quarterly Review*, and other journals. Her first book, *The Patience of the Cloud Photographer*, was published in 1997 by Carnegie Mellon University Press.

FANNY HOWE is the author of over twenty books of poetry and fiction, including *Saving History, Famous Questions*, and *The Quietist*. She is a professor of writing and American literature at the University of California, San Diego.

MARY KARR is the author of the best-selling memoir *The Liars' Club* and three collections of poems, *Abacus, The Devil's Tour,* and *Viper Rum,* which was published this past spring by New Directions.

MAURICE KILWEIN GUEVARA's poem in this issue is from a recently completed book of prose poems, *Autobiography of So-and-so.* His other books include *Postmortem* (Georgia, 1994) and *Poems of the River Spirit* (Pittsburgh, 1996). His work also appears in Ray Gonzalez's anthology *Touching the Fire: Fifteen Poets of Today's Latino Renaissance* (Anchor/Doubleday, 1998).

STEVE KOWIT is the author of *In the Palm of Your Hand: The Poet's Portable Workshop.* His most recent collection is *Epic Journeys, Unbelievable Escapes,* from State Street Press. He lives in the Southern California backcountry near the Mexican border.

ADRIAN C. LOUIS teaches on the Pine Ridge Reservation of South Dakota. His most recent book of poems is *Ceremonies of the Damned* (Nevada, 1997). A new chapbook, *Skull Dance,* is available from Bull Thistle Press in Jamaica, Vermont.

SUZANNE LUMMIS teaches poetry through UCLA Extension, and received their Outstanding Teacher Award in 1996. She is a founding member of the experimental performance troupe *Nearly Fatal Women,* and the editor of *Grand Passion: The Poets of Los Angeles and Beyond.* Recent poems appear in *Solo* and *Poetry Flash.*

R. J. MCCAFFERY is a poet and reviewer who lives and works in Providence, Rhode Island. He may be contacted at rjmccaffery@geocities.com.

JEFFREY MCDANIEL is the author of *Alibi School* and *The Forgiveness Parade,* both from Manic D Press. His poems have appeared in *New (American) Poets, Best American Poetry 1994,* and on NPR's "Talk of the Nation" and a CNN special on poetry slams. He is seeking a publisher for an anthology project, *A Tongue in Both Ears,* featuring performance poets of the nineties whose work stands on the page. He lives in Los Angeles, where he works as a freelance writer and a teacher.

H. BRUCE MCEVER has taken poetry workshops at Sarah Lawrence College with Thomas Lux and Kevin Pilkington and in New York City with Brooks Haxton, J. D. McClatchy, David Lehman, Hugh Seidman, Katha Pollitt, and Pearl London. He is also the president of Berkshire Capital Corporation, an investment banking firm in New York City. He and his wife live on a farm in Salisbury, Connecticut.

CAMPBELL MCGRATH won *Ploughshares'* 1997 Cohen Award for Best Poem. The poem in this issue is from his new book, *Road Atlas,* forthcoming from Ecco Press in 1999.

WESLEY MCNAIR's fifth book of poems, *Talking in the Dark,* was published this past fall by David R. Godine, which also reprinted *The Town of No; & My Brother Running* in 1997. He received the 1997 Sarah Josepha Hale Medal for his "distinguished contribution to the world of letters."

JOSHUA MEHIGAN lives in Brooklyn, New York, and works as an online editor. His poems have appeared in *The Formalist, Verse, Pequod, Pivot,* and other journals. His work was nominated for inclusion in *The Pushcart Prize XXIII. Confusing Weather,* a chapbook, was printed this year by Black Cat Press.

ORLANDO RICARDO MENES is a Cuban American who teaches English and creative writing at the University of Illinois in Chicago. New poems have recently appeared or are forthcoming in *The Antioch Review, Chelsea, The Indiana Review,* and *Callaloo.* His second poetry collection, *Rumba Atop the Stones,* is being considered by a number of presses.

W. S. MERWIN is the author of more than fifteen books of poetry, including *The Folding Cliffs, Flower and Hand: Poems 1977–1983, The Vixen, Travels,* and *The Carrier of Ladders,* which won a Pulitzer Prize. He has also published numerous plays, nearly twenty books of translation, and four books of prose, including *The Lost Upland,* his memoir of life in the south of France. He lives in Hawaii.

GEORGE MILLS, who passed away this summer, was the author of several books of poems, including *The House Sails Out of Sight of Home,* which won the 1991 Morse Poetry Prize.

JUDITH MOORE has been the recipient of fellowships from the Guggenheim Foundation and twice from the NEA. She is co-author with Sue Coe of *X,* and author of *The Left Coast of Paradise.* Her essay collection, *Never Eat Your Heart Out,* was published in 1997. She is an editor and staff writer for *The San Diego Reader.* She lives in Berkeley, California.

KIRK NESSET's poems and stories have recently appeared in *The Paris Review, The Iowa Review, The Gettysburg Review, The Antioch Review, The Boston Review, Prairie Schooner, Zyzzyva,* and elsewhere. His story "Mr. Agreeable," published last year in *Fiction,* was selected for *The Pushcart Prize XXI.* His nonfiction study, *The Stories of Raymond Carver,* was published in 1995 by the Ohio University Press. He teaches creative writing at Allegheny College.

STEVE ORLEN's most recent book is *Kisses* (Miami, 1997). He teaches at the University of Arizona in Tucson and at Warren Wilson College's M.F.A. Program for Writers.

MAUREEN PILKINGTON, after working in book publishing as a subsidiary rights director, received her M.F.A. from Sarah Lawrence College in 1997. Her most recent story appeared in the Spring issue of *Santa Barbara Review.* She is currently working on a collection of short stories and lives in Rye, New York.

ROBIN REAGLER lives in Houston, Texas. Her poems have appeared in *The Colorado Review, ACM (Another Chicago Magazine), Denver Quarterly, The Iowa Review,* and other journals. She is Executive Director of Writers in the Schools (WITS).

CLENN REED has had poems published in *Ploughshares, The Alaska Quarterly Review,* and several other periodicals. He was a recent winner of the Aldrich Museum Emerging Poets Reading Series. He lives in New York City, where he teaches writing at Sarah Lawrence College, Long Island University, and Mercy College.

KIRSTIN M. ROEHRICH recently received her M.F.A. from Emerson College, where she studied with Bill Knott. She lives in Pittsburgh.

FRAZIER RUSSELL is Assistant Director and a core faculty member of The Writers Studio, a private school for writers based in Manhattan. His poems have appeared in *The American Voice, Global City Review,* and other journals. In 1996, his chapbook novella, *Fweivel: The Day Will Come,* was published by Ridgeway Press.

MICHAEL RYAN's autobiography, *Secret Life,* was a *New York Times* Notable Book for 1995. Among the many awards he has won for his poetry are the Yale Series of Younger Poets Award, fellowships from the NEA and Guggenheim Foundation, a Whiting Writer's Award, the Lenore Marshall/*The Nation* Award, and the Cohen Award from *Ploughshares.*

NATASHA SAJÉ is the author of *Red Under the Skin* (Pittsburgh, 1994) and essays in *The Henry James Review, The American Voice,* and *Legacy: Journal of American Women Writers.* She teaches at Westminster College of Salt Lake City and in the M.F.A. in Writing Program of Vermont College.

FAITH SHEARIN teaches high-school English at Cranbrook Schools outside Detroit. Her poems have appeared in numerous journals, including *The Iowa Woman, The Alaska Quarterly Review, New York Quarterly, The Charlotte Poetry Review,* and *The Chicago Review.* She was a fellow at the Fine Arts Work Center in Provincetown, where she later served on the Writing Committee, and was the 1996 Writer-in-Residence at the Interlochen Arts Academy.

EVA SKRANDE lives in Houston.

BRUCE SMITH is the author of three books of poems. A new collection, *The Other Lover,* is forthcoming from the University of Chicago Press. He teaches at the University of Alabama in Tuscaloosa.

TERESA STARR was born in Kentucky and currently lives in New York State.

MARC J. STRAUS has recent or forthcoming poems in *The Kenyon Review, Tri-Quarterly, The Virginia Quarterly Review,* and elsewhere. His first collection of poetry, *One Word,* was published by TriQuarterly/Northwestern University Press in 1994, and his second collection, *Not God,* is due out from Northwestern in 1999. He received The Robert Penn Warren Award from Yale University Medical School in 1998. He runs a medical oncology practice in White Plains, New York.

TERESE SVOBODA is the author of a novel, *Cannibal,* and three collections of poetry, *Laughing Africa, All Aberration,* and *Mere Mortals.* A new novel, *A Drink Called Paradise,* is forthcoming from Counterpoint Press.

WISLAWA SZYMBORSKA was born in 1923 in Kórnik, Poland. She started publishing shortly after World War II, and has received the Goethe Prize, the

Herder Prize, and the 1996 Nobel Prize for Literature. She lives in Krakow, Poland, where she enjoys making collages for friends.

DANIEL TOBIN grew up in Brooklyn, New York, and currently teaches at Carthage College and at The School of the Art Institute of Chicago. His work has appeared in many journals, among them *Poetry, DoubleTake, The National Forum,* and *The Tampa Review.* He was awarded the Discovery/*The Nation* Award in 1995, and an NEA fellowship in 1996. His book of poems, *Where the World Is Made,* won the 1998 Bakeless Prize.

JOANNA TRZECIAK has been an authorized translator for Wislawa Szymborska since 1989. Her translations have appeared in *The New Yorker, The Times Literary Supplement, Poetry, Harper's, The Atlantic Monthly,* and *The Paris Review.* She is currently at work on a collection of her translations of Szymborska's poetry. Her translation of Tomek Tryzna's novel *Panna Nikt (Miss Nobody)* is scheduled to be published by Doubleday this winter. She is a doctoral student in Russian Literature at the University of Chicago.

PETER TURCHI is the author of a novel, *The Girls Next Door,* a collection of stories, *Magician,* and a book of nonfiction. The recipient of an NEA fellowship, North Carolina's Sir Walter Raleigh Prize, and an Illinois Arts Council Literary Award, he teaches in and serves as Director of Warren Wilson College's M.F.A. Program for Writers.

LEE UPTON's third book of poems, *Approximate Darling,* appeared in 1996 from the University of Alabama Press. Her third book of criticism, *The Muse of Abandonment: Origin, Identity, Mastery in Five American Poets,* was published by Bucknell University Press this fall.

MATHEW R. WEAVER lives in Brooklyn, New York. His work has been exhibited in New York, Ohio, Canada, The Netherlands, Germany, and Switzerland, and is included in numerous private collections in the U.S. and Europe. He has been an artist-in-residence at The Millay Colony, Yaddo, and Anderson Ranch Arts Center.

CHARLES HARPER WEBB is a rock singer turned psychotherapist and professor of English at California State University, Long Beach. His first book, *Reading the Water* (Northeastern), won the 1997 Morse Poetry Prize and the 1998 Kate Tufts Discovery Award.

～

HOW IT WORKS *Ploughshares* is published three times a year: mixed issues of poetry and fiction in the Spring and Winter and a fiction issue in the Fall, with each guest-edited by a different writer of prominence, usually one whose early work was published in the journal. Guest editors are invited to solicit up to half of their issues, with the other half comprised of unsolicited manuscripts screened for them by staff editors. This guest-editor policy is designed to introduce readers to different literary circles and tastes, and to offer a fuller representation of the range and diversity of contemporary letters than would be possible with a single editorship. Yet, at the same time, we expect every issue to reflect our overall standards of literary excellence. We liken *Ploughshares* to a theater company: each issue might have a different guest editor and different writers— just as a play will have a different director, playwright, and cast—but subscribers can count on a governing aesthetic, a consistency in literary values and quality, that is uniquely our own.

SUBMISSION POLICIES We welcome unsolicited manuscripts from August 1 to March 31 (postmark dates). All submissions sent from April to July are returned unread. In the past, guest editors often announced specific themes for issues, but we have revised our editorial policies and no longer restrict submissions to thematic topics. Submit your work at any time during our reading period; if a manuscript is not timely for one issue, it will be considered for another. We do not recommend trying to target specific guest editors. Our backlog is unpredictable, and staff editors ultimately have the responsibility of determining for which editor a work is most appropriate. Send one prose piece and/or one to three poems at a time (mail genres separately). Poems should be individually typed either single- or double-spaced on one side of the page. Prose should be typed double-spaced on one side and be no longer than twenty-five pages. Although we look primarily for short stories, we occasionally publish personal essays/memoirs. Novel excerpts are acceptable if self-contained. Unsolicited book reviews and criticism are not considered. Please do not send multiple submissions of the same genre, and do not send another manuscript until you hear about the first. Additional submissions will be returned unread. No more than a total of two submissions per reading period, please. Mail your manuscript in a page-size manila envelope, your full name and address written on the outside, to the "Fiction Editor," "Poetry Editor," or "Nonfiction Editor." Unsolicited work sent directly to a guest editor's home or office will be ignored and discarded; guest editors are formally instructed not to read such work. All manuscripts and correspondence regarding submissions should be accompanied by a self-addressed, stamped envelope (s.a.s.e.) for a response. Expect three to five months for a decision. Do not query us until five months have passed, and if you do, please write to us, including an s.a.s.e. and indicating the postmark date of submission, instead of calling. Simultaneous submissions are amenable as long as they are indicated as such and we are notified immediately upon acceptance elsewhere. We cannot accommodate revisions, changes of return address, or forgotten s.a.s.e.'s after the fact. We do not reprint previously published work. Translations are welcome if permission has been granted. We cannot be responsible for delay, loss, or damage. Payment is upon publication: $25/printed page, $50 minimum per title, $250 maximum per author, with two copies of the issue and a one-year subscription.

INDEX TO VOLUME XXIV

Ploughshares · A Journal of New Writing · 1998

Ploughshares Donors

With great gratitude, we would like to acknowledge the following readers who generously made donations to *Ploughshares* during our 1998 fund-raising campaign.

Anonymous (15)
Sharon Anson
Leo Baefsky
Henry Berne
Sheila Bjornlie
Sally Bradlee
Sylvia K. Burack
  The Writer Magazine
Jean Burden
Virginia Cadden
Kathleen Chadwick
Richard F. Concannon
Bonnie Connors
Susan DeWitt Davie
Tim Dirkx
Lynn Emanuel
Seymour Epstein
Barbara P. Erdle
Marilyn Ferrari
Charles C. Foster
Norton Girault
Joline Gitis
Joanne Goodrich
Ann S. Graham
Joy Harjo
Stacey Harper
Steve Haskin
James Haug
William Locke Hauser
Seamus Heaney
Faye M. Hoyal
Alice Kenner
Galway Kinnell
Joseph Kostolefsky

Maxine Kumin
David Lehman
In Memory of Larry Levis
  and William Matthews
Irish Books & Media
Patricia Lee Lewis
Harold and Edith Lohr
Suzanne Lummis
Fred Marchant
James E. Marsh
Cleopatra Mathis
Alice Mattison
Margaret Michaels
Kenneth Mintz
Judith H. Montgomery
Linda Neal Reising
Grace S. Roman
Donald and Barbara
  Romano
Ron Samul, Jr.
Rosalind A. Sibielski
Deborah Silverman
Carol Houck Smith
Gary Soto
Amelia Stafford
Maura Stanton
Clara Stites
Joanne Trafton
Barbara Tran
Gale Ward
Michael Warshaw
Sarah Wilson
Cynthia Wyatt

THE BOSTON BOOK REVIEW

http://www.BostonBookReview.com

The Best of Both Worlds

The Apollonian

The Bostonian

The Dionysian

The thinking person's literary arts magazine with fiction, poetry, interviews, essays and book reviews.

Subscribe to the BOSTON BOOK REVIEW.
Discover the well-written.

In addition, sign up to receive our **FREE** bimonthly email Gazette for info about authors, new articles and reviews, BBR bestsellers and best picks, occasional short reviews, and more. Send an email with **subscribe** in the subject line to Gazette@soapbox.BostonBookReview.com.

SUBSCRIPTIONS: 1 yr. (10 issues) $24.00   plshr
Canada and International add $26.00

Name _____

Address_____

City _____State _____Zip _____

Credit Card Payments: No. _____
or call (617) 497-0344   Exp. date:_____ Signature: _____
☐ VISA   ☐ MASTERCARD   ☐ DISCOVER   ☐ AMEX

Or send check to:
THE BOSTON BOOK REVIEW, 30 Brattle Street, 4th floor, Cambridge, MA 02138

WORDSWORTH
Discounts on Every*Book, Every Day

Edited by Garrison Keillor, this years volume features work by John Updike, Meg Wolitzer, Lorrie Moore, Matthew Crain and Annie Proulx among others.

(Houghton Mifflin)
List Price: $13.00
Our Price: $11.70

The Best American Essays 1998 features a mix of people and prose, as guest editor Cynthia Ozick shapes a volume around the intricacies of human memory. With work by Saul Bellow, Jamaica Kincaid, Andre Dubois, John McPhee, John Updike and many others.

(Houghton Mifflin)
List Price: $13.00
Our Price: $11.70

WORDSWORTH
BOOKS
30 Brattle St., Harvard Sq.,Cambridge
(800) 899-2202 ~ Fax# (617) 354-4674
www.wordsworth.com

*Except textbooks

NEW FROM GRAYWOLF PRESS

Nola: A Memoir of Faith, Art, and Madness

ROBIN HEMLEY

"Hemley's book sits square in the center of the new and most successful nonfiction, exemplifying the trend of stretching the form. *Nola* is not just a life-and-death narrative of the author's brilliant and disturbed sister, but it's also a complex narrative of Hemley himself, of his mother as writer and editor, and finally it is the story of how he makes meaning out of his own connections with his difficult, eccentric and excruciatingly literary family."   *ForeWord*

Hardcover, $24.95 (1-55597-278-0)

Crossing the Expendable Landscape

Essays by BETTINA DREW

Drew takes the reader on an exploration of several American cities—Stamford, Branson, Hilton Head, Las Vegas, Dallas, Celebration—to examine the consequences of built environments that fail to reflect regional, historic, and social values.

"[Drew's] criticism is sharp-edged, to the point, and nearly inarguable....A solid, well-argued, and sometimes radical plea for a better-built environment."
Kirkus Reviews

Paperback, $15.00 (1-55597-279-9)

Relations: New and Selected Poems

EAMON GRENNAN

"In Grennan's best poems, and there are many in this collection, the precision of his observations renders the embodied lives of others with gripping lucidity."
Publishers Weekly

"Few poets are as generous as Eamon Grennan in the sheer volume of delight his poems convey, and fewer still are as attentive to the available marvels of the earth. To read him is to be led on a walk through the natural world of clover and cricket and, most of all, light, and to face with an open heart the complexity of being human."   *Billy Collins*

Paperback, $16.00 (1-55597-280-2)

GRAYWOLF PRESS
2402 University Avenue, Suite 203 · St. Paul, MN 55114
651-641-0077 · FAX: 651-641-0036
www.graywolfpress.org

NEW FROM GRAYWOLF PRESS

Central Square

GEORGE PACKER

"Packer has a good feel for the sunlight-deficient lives of a typical New England winter, but the novel is more than a few deft portraits of selected urban existence. It is a graceful meditation on the moral longing and often doomed effort that go into reinventing oneself." *Publishers Weekly*

Hardcover, $24.95 (1-55597-277-2)

Readings

Essays by SVEN BIRKERTS

This collection encompasses the best of cultural and literary critic Sven Birkerts, who discusses authors ranging from Robert Musil to Don DeLillo, questions the influence of technology upon sensibility, and probes our contemporary sense of time and place.

Paperback, $16.00 (1-55597-283-7) Available February 1999

Take Three: 3

AGNI *New Poets Series*

Edited by ASKOLD MELNYCZUK

Jennifer Barber, Mark Bibbins, and Maggie Nelson are featured in this new volume of the Take Three series, which is designed to launch the work of exciting young poets. In a review of *Take Three:1, Booklist* declared that, "This satisfying sampler makes one hope the series it begins continues for many years."

Paperback, $12.95 (1-55597-282-9)

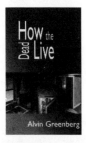

How the Dead Live

ALVIN GREENBERG

"Death, disguised as a rabbi, gets stuck in traffic in one of Alvin Greenberg's remarkable stories. Eerie, wry, and humane, these tales are both comforting and unsettling, because they bring us the darkest news with great equanimity. There is another side to everything, including mortality, and Alvin Greenberg seems to have been there and brought these stories back." *Charles Baxter*

Paperback, $14.00 (1-55597-281-0)

GRAYWOLF PRESS
2402 University Avenue, Suite 203 · St. Paul, MN 55114
651-641-0077 · FAX: 651-641-0036
www.graywolfpress.org

THE GREENSBORO REVIEW

For Over 30 Years
A Publisher of Poetry & Fiction

Works from the journal have been anthologized or cited in *Best American Short Stories, Prize Stories: The O. Henry Awards, Pushcart Prize, New Stories from the South,* and other collections honoring the finest new writing.

Recent Contributors

A. Manette Ansay
Stephen Dobyns
Brendan Galvin
Richard Garcia
Rodney Jones

Jean Ross Justice
Thomas Lux
Jill McCorkle
Peter Meinke
Robert Morgan

Robert Olmstead
Dale Ray Phillips
David Rivard
Tom Sleigh
Eleanor Ross Taylor

Subscriptions

Sample copy—$5   One year—$10   Three years—$25

The Greensboro Review
English Department, UNCG
PO Box 26170
Greensboro, NC 27402-6170

Visit our website
www.uncg.edu/eng/mfa
or send SASE for deadlines
and submission guidelines

Produced by the MFA Writing Program at Greensboro

Waxing Poetic

Paris

POEMS BY JIM BARNES

"Barnes writes for the reader and the wayfarer, for the lonely artist craving inspiration and the traveler courting experience." — *The Virginia Quarterly Review*

Paper, $16.95

The Rooster Mask

POEMS BY HENRY HART

"Remarkable for its range and expressiveness. Hart emerges here as one of the best poets of his generation." — Jay Parini, author of *Benjamin's Crossing* and *Robert Frost: A Biography*

Paper, $14.95

Lost Wax

POEMS BY HEATHER RAMSDELL

"A metaphysical treasure hunt, here a stick, there a door, a closet, a shirt.... a symphony of poems that is original and profoundly full of wonder." — James Tate

National Poetry Series

Paper, $11.95

The Trouble-Making Finch

POEMS BY LEN ROBERTS

"A poet of unwavering truthfulness and unwavering mercy—somehow the mercy always equal to the truth." — Sharon Olds

Paper, $14.95

Grazing

POEMS BY IRA SADOFF

"A tentative, moody toughness runs through Sadoff's poems, wrenching them into odd shapes, and showing the poet to be suspicious of epiphany even as he courts it.... Many of the poems here drift on a tide of bitter retrospection." — *Publishers Weekly*

Paper, $12.95

The Wild Card

Selected Poems, Early and Late

KARL SHAPIRO

Edited by Stanley Kunitz and David Ignatow
Introduction by M. L. Rosenthal. Foreword by Stanley Kunitz

"Shapiro's early work includes excellent formal lyrics ... and demonstrates a verbal virtuosity worthy of Auden, Shapiro's acknowledged master.... Welcome back to the limelight, Mr. Shapiro!" — *Booklist**

Cloth, $26.95; Paper, $18.95

"I Cease Not to Yowl"

Ezra Pound's Letters to Olivia Rossetti Agresti

EDITED BY DEMETRES P. TRYPHONOPOULOS AND LEON SURETTE

"This correspondence is a gold mine.... It tells an important story—one with profound cultural and political implications." — Marjorie Perloff, author of *The Dance of the Intellect*

Illus. Cloth, $34.95

The Ways We Touch

POEMS BY MILLER WILLIAMS

"Williams is gifted with a view of ordinary life relieved of illusion and sentimentality.... In these memorable poems, Miller Williams adds to our store of wisdom of literature." — *The Hudson Review*

Cloth, $16.95

(800) 545-4703 • UNIVERSITY OF ILLINOIS PRESS• www.press.uillinois.edu/subject/poe.html

Indiana University Writers' Conference

Catherine Bowman	Jesse Lee Kercheval	Barbara Shoup
Rodney Jones	Brad Leithauser	Jon Tribble
Allison Joseph	Manny Martinez	Charles Webb
	Mary Jo Salter	

June 27th through July 2nd

Join some of the country's top writers for a week of workshops, readings, classes, and panel discussions. The conference is comfortably situated on the wooded campus of Indiana University in Bloomington, Indiana.

For information & an application, call or write:

Ballantine Hall 464, Indiana University
Bloomington, Indiana 47405. (812) 855-1877
http://php.indiana.edu/~iuwc/

THIS PUBLICATION AVAILABLE FROM UMI

This publication is available from UMI in one or more of the following formats:

- **In Microform**--from our collection of over 18,000 periodicals and 7,000 newspapers

- **In Paper**--by the article or full issues through UMI Article Clearinghouse

- **Electronically, on CD-ROM, online, and/or magnetic tape**--a broad range of ProQuest databases available, including abstract-and-index, ASCII full-text, and innovative full-image format

Call toll-free 800-521-0600, ext. 2888, for more information, or fill out the coupon below:

Name ————————————————————
Title ————————————————————
Company/Institution ————————————————
Address ——————————————————————
City/State/Zip ————————————————————
Phone (   ) ————————————————————
I'm interested in the following title(s): ———————————

UMI
A Bell & Howell Company
Box 78
300 North Zeeb Road
Ann Arbor, MI 48106

800-521-0600 toll-free
313-761-1203 fax

UMI

Sarah Lawrence College
MFA in Writing

An intensive program combining small seminar workshops and biweekly private conferences with faculty.*

Fiction

Linsey Abrams
Melvin Jules Bukiet
Peter Cameron
Carolyn Ferrell
Myra Goldberg
Kathleen Hill
Gale Jackson
Fenton Johnson
William Melvin Kelley
Mary LaChapelle
Brian Morton
Lucy Rosenthal
Joan Silber
Brooke Stevens
Susan Thames

Nonfiction

Mary Morris
Barbara Probst Solomon
Laurence Weschler

Poetry

Billy Collins
Suzanne Gardinier
Marie Howe
Kate Knapp Johnson
Joan Larkin
Thomas Lux
Tracie Morris
Kevin Pilkington
Victoria Redel
Vijay Seshadri
Gerald Stern
Jean Valentine

*1998-99 faculty

Write or call **Graduate Studies,**
Sarah Lawrence College, Box S
1 Mead Way
Bronxville, NY 10708-5999
Tel: (914) 395-2373
or e-mail: grad@mail.slc.edu
Full and part-time study available.

M.F.A. in
Creative Writing

M.A. in
Writing & Publishing

Located in historic Boston, right on
"The Common," Emerson College
offers an exciting community for
writers and aspiring publishers.
Home to the nationally renowned
journal *Ploughshares*, Emerson's
graduate program nurtures new
voices and provides diverse
opportunities for study in an
environment of discovery and
growth. Class sizes are small, with
enrollments limited to twelve
students in workshops.

Graduate Admission
100 Beacon Street
Boston, MA 02116
Tel: (617) 824-8610
Fax: (617) 824-8614
gradapp@emerson.edu
www.emerson.edu/gradapp

EMERSON
COLLEGE

*Current Faculty in the
Department of Writing,
Literature & Publishing:*

John Skoyles, Chair
Jonathan Aaron
Douglas Clayton
William Donoghue
Robin Riley Fast
Eileen Farrell
Flora Gonzalez
Lisa Jahn-Clough
DeWitt Henry
Christopher Keane
Maria Koundoura
Bill Knott
Margot Livesey
Ralph Lombreglia
Gail Mazur
Tracy McCabe
Pamela Painter
Donald Perret
Michael Stephens
Christopher Tilghman

Adjunct Faculty include:

David Barber, Sam
Cornish, Andre Dubus III,
Marcie Hershman, William
Holinger, Kai Maristed,
George Packer, Martha
Rhodes, Elizabeth Searle,
Jessica Treadway

Concentrations in:

Fiction, Poetry,
Non-Fiction,
Screenwriting,
Children's Literature,
& Publishing

BENNINGTON WRITING SEMINARS

MFA in Writing and Literature
Two-Year Low-Residency Program

A. BLAKE GARDNER

FICTION
NONFICTION
POETRY

Jane Kenyon Poetry Scholarships available
For more information contact:
Writing Seminars
Box PL
Bennington College
Bennington, VT 05201
802-440-4452, Fax 802-447-4269

FACULTY
FICTION
Douglas Bauer
Elizabeth Cox
Susan Dodd
Maria Flook
Lynn Freed
Amy Hempel
Alice Mattison
Jill McCorkle
Askold Melnyczuk
Rick Moody

NONFICTION
Sven Birkerts
Susan Cheever
Lucy Grealy
Bob Shacochis

POETRY
April Bernard
Thomas Sayers Ellis
David Lehman
Jane Hirshfield
Carol Muske
Liam Rector
Jason Shinder

POET-IN-RESIDENCE
Donald Hall

RECENT ASSOCIATE
FACULTY
Robert Bly
Lucie Brock-Broido
Karen Finley
Marie Howe
Carole Maso
Howard Norman
Robert Pinsky
Roger Shattuck
Tom Wicker

If your book isn't here, it will be.

Custom Book Ordering Made Easy

At Harvard Book Store, we pride ourselves on the depth and diversity of the books on our shelves, and hope you won't need our customer order department. But we also pride ourselves on the ever-changing and eclectic needs of our cus-

Your Book

*tomers. So, **if you can't find the book you need, we can**. We have a select staff dedicated to your orders. Harvard Book Store customer orders rarely take more than two weeks. In fact, most U.S. books arrive within a few days.*

Harvard Book Store

1256 Massachusetts Ave.   (617) 661-1515

http://www.harvard.com   E-mail: hbs-info@harvard.com

MFA in

Poetry
Fiction
Creative Non-Fiction

At Mills *we are a community of writers
and scholars who work with words.
We have what writers need: a remarkable
faculty, distinguished visiting writers,
small workshops, and a personalized
program focusing on the individual
student— all on a beautiful campus in
the literary hotbed of the San Francisco
Bay Area.*

The place for writers is here.

*To learn more, contact the Graduate Office
for application information:*

*Graduate Office
Mills College
5000 MacArthur Blvd.
Oakland, CA 94613
510-430-3309*

■ 2-Year MA in literature,
MFA in creative writing.
Attractive 135-acre
campus; residence option;
some financial aid

■ **CORE FACULTY**
Elmaz Abinader
Chana Bloch
Stephen Ratcliffe

■ **WRITERS IN RESIDENCE**
Toi Dericotte
Cristina Garcia
Ginu Kamani
Cecile Pineda
Kathryn Reiss
Elizabeth Willis

■ **DISTINGUISHED VISITORS**
Dorothy Allison
Kathleen Fraser
Tess Gallagher
Louise Glück
Barbara Guest
Janet Campbell Hale
Fanny Howe
Ishmael Reed
Adrienne Rich
Leslie Scalapino
Julie Shigekuni

community

MILLS. *In a word.*

Ploughshares

a literary adventure

Known for its compelling fiction and poetry, *Ploughshares* is widely regarded as one of America's most influential literary journals. Each issue is guest-edited by a different writer for a fresh, provocative slant— exploring personal visions, aesthetics, and literary circles—and contributors include both well-known and emerging writers. In fact, *Ploughshares* has become a premier proving ground for new talent, showcasing the early works of Sue Miller, Mona Simpson, Robert Pinsky, and countless others. Past guest editors include Richard Ford, Derek Walcott, Tobias Wolff, Carolyn Forché, and Rosellen Brown. This unique editorial format has made *Ploughshares,* in effect, into a dynamic anthology series—one that has established a tradition of quality and prescience. *Ploughshares* is published in quality trade paperback in April, August, and December: usually a fiction issue in the Fall and mixed issues of poetry and fiction in the Spring and Winter. Inside each issue, you'll find not only great new stories and poems, but also a profile on the guest editor, book reviews, and miscellaneous notes about *Ploughshares,* its writers, and the literary world. Subscribe today.

Sample *Ploughshares* on the Web: http://www.emerson.edu/ploughshares

- -

❏ **Send me a one-year subscription for $21.**
I save $8.85 off the cover price (3 issues).

❏ **Send me a two-year subscription for $40.**
I save $19.70 off the cover price (6 issues).

Start with: ❏ Spring ❏ Fall ❏ Winter

Add $5 per year for international. Institutions: $24.

Name_____

Address _____

_____

Mail with check to: Ploughshares · Emerson College
100 Beacon St. · Boston, MA 02116